KU-665-665

European Poetry
In Scotland

European Poetry
In Scotland

AN ANTHOLOGY OF
TRANSLATIONS

Edited by
Peter France & Duncan Glen

EDINBURGH UNIVERSITY PRESS

© Edinburgh University Press 1989
22 George Square, Edinburgh

Set in Linotron Palatino by
Hewer Text Composition Edinburgh
and printed in Great Britain by
Redwood Burn Limited,
Trowbridge, Wilts

British Library Cataloguing
  in Publication Data
European poetry in Scotland an anthology of
  translations.
  I. France, Peter   II. Glen, Duncan
  808.81
  ISBN 0 85224 624 2
  ISBN 0 85224 625 0 pbk

The publisher acknowledges subsidy
from the Scottish Arts Council towards
the publication of this volume.

Contents

Acknowledgements

Our thanks for help generously given are due to the staffs of
the Scottish Poetry Library, the Scottish Library of Edinburgh
Central Public Library, the National Library of Scotland
and the University of Edinburgh Library.

For permission to print the translations in this book, thanks are due to
the following:

J. K. Annand and Akros Publications for poems from *Poems and
Translations*; Robin Bell and Maria Blasquez for previously unpublished
poems; Mrs Marianne Bowman and Tamarind Press for poem from *Out
of My System*, and the editors of *Cencrastus* and *Scottish International* for
other poems; Ronald Butlin and Edinburgh University Student Publica-
tions Board for poems from *Creatures Tamed by Cruelty* and the editor of
Aquarius for other poems; Robert Calder for previously unpublished
poem; Donald Campbell and Akros Publications for poem from *Blether*;
Robert Crawford for previously unpublished poems; Douglas Dunn and
Edinburgh University Press for poem from *A Scottis Quair* and the editor
of *The International Portland Review* for other poems; Alastair Fowler and
Edinburgh University Press for poems from *A Scottis Quair*; Peter France,
Jon Stallworthy and Allen Lane, Publishers for poem from *Boris
Pasternak: Selected Poems*, and Cambridge University Press for poems
from *Poets of Modern Russia* and Peter France for previously unpublished
poems; Mrs Eileen Fraser and Leicester University Press for poems from
Poems of G. S. Fraser; Robin Fulton and Anvil Press Poetry Ltd for poems
from *Don't Give Me the Whole Truth: Selected Poems of Olav Hauge*, and
Brigham Young University for poems from *Towards the Solitary Star:
Selected Poetry and Prose of Östen Sjöstrand*, and Bloodaxe Books for poems
from *Collected Poems: Tomas Tranströmer*; the executors of Robert Garioch
Sutherland and Macdonald Publishers Edinburgh for poems from *Robert
Garioch: Complete Poems*; Valerie Gillies for previously unpublished
poem; Duncan Glen and Akros Publications for poems from *The State of
Scotland* and Duncan Glen for previously unpublished poems; Mr John
Gray for poems by Sir Alexander Gray; the trustees of the W. L. Lorimer
Memorial Trust and the holder of the copyright for poems by George
Campbell Hay; Hamish Henderson and the editors of *Chapman* and *New
Road* for poems; the literary executor of J. F. Hendry for previously
unpublished poems; W. N. Herbert and Obog Books for the poem from
Sterts and Stobies and W. N. Herbert for previously unpublished poem;
Tom Hubbard and the editors of *Scottish Slavonic Review* and *Scrievins* for
poems; Alexander Hutchison and the editors of *Chapman*, *Lallans* and
Verse for poems and Alexander Hutchison for unpublished poems;
George Kay and Edinburgh University Press for poems with *Montale:*

Poesie/Poems, and the editor of *Lines Review* for other poem; George MacBeth for extract from his poem; Michael Grieve and Martin Brian & O'Keeffe and Penguin Books Ltd for poems from *The Complete Poems of Hugh MacDiarmid*; Alastair Mackie and Edinburgh University Press for poems from *A Scottis Quair* and the editor of *Akros* for poems and Alastair Mackie for previously unpublished poems; John Manson and the editor of *Weighbauk* for poems; Graham Dunstan Martin and Edinburgh University Press for poems from *Louise Labé: Sonnets* and *Anthology of Contemporary French Poetry*; William Montgomerie and Canongate Publishing Ltd for poems from *From Time to Time*; Edwin Morgan and Carcanet Press for poems from *Rites of Passage* and *Wi the Haill Voice*, Whiteknights Press, University of Reading, for poems from *Fifty Renascence Love-Poems*, and Anvil Press Poetry Ltd for poems from *Eternal Moment: Selected Poems by Sándor Weöres* and the editors of *Cencrastus*, *Lallans* and *Scottish Slavonic Review* for other poems; William Neill and Gordon Wright Publishing for poems from *Making Tracks*; Tessa Ransford for previously unpublished poems; Alexander Scott and Akros Publications for poem from *Selected Poems 1943–1974*; Tom Scott and Oxford University Press for poems from *The Ship and ither poems*, and the editor of *Agenda* for poems, and Tom Scott for other poems; the literary executor of Burns Singer for poem; Mrs Hazel Goodsir Smith and John Calder (Publishers) Ltd for poems from *Collected Poems 1941–1975*; the Trustees of the National Library of Scotland for poems by William Soutar; Antonia Stott and the editor of *Scottish International* for poems; William J. Tait and Paul Harris Publishing for poems from *A Day Between Weathers* and the editor of *Lallans* for other poem; Roderick Watson and the editor of *Lines Review* for poems; Christopher Whyte for previously unpublished poems; Miss Clara Young for poems by Douglas Young.

We have sought to identify all copyright-holders to the best of our ability. If in any case we have inadvertently failed to do so, we offer our apologies and would be grateful to be informed of the omission.

Individual copyright in all the poems printed here remains with the original holder.

Introduction

This is a collection of European poetry translated by twentieth-century Scottish poets and others living in Scotland and playing a part in the cultural life of the country. However, as a bow of acknowledgement to one of the great translators of world literature, who is also the father of Scottish translation, we have printed as a prologue a brief extract from Gavin Douglas's *Eneados*. Douglas's example was followed, both in Scots and in English, by some of the great poets of the first Scottish Renaissance, notably Drummond of Hawthornden. Thereafter, although Allan Ramsay, for instance, produced versions of Horace, La Motte and La Fontaine, it is hardly an exaggeration to say that no important translations of poetry were produced in Scotland until the work of Sir Alexander Gray and Hugh MacDiarmid in the twenties of the present century. It is with them that our story really begins.

In the Renaissance period, in several European countries, translation from the Classics had served to launch vernacular literatures on the road of autonomous dignity. For Ronsard and Du Bellay, for instance, French poetry had to look to the classics, not always in slavish imitation, but as an escape from limited provincialism. At about the same time, many of the European languages and literatures attained adulthood by becoming (through translation) the language of their culture's sacred text, the Bible. As we know, centuries were to pass before Scotland had its own Biblical translation.

A new Renaissance came. Like Ronsard looking to the classics, Hugh MacDiarmid had as one of his principal aims to take Scottish poetry back into the mainstream of European poetry, looking beyond England to the continent. In the *Dunfermline Press* of 5 August 1922 he wrote: 'If there is to be a Scottish literary revival, the first essential is to get rid of our provinciality of outlook and to avail ourselves of Continental experience'. His translations of the twenties into both Scots and English are a part of this campaign. One of the aims of his most influential magazine, *The Scottish Chapbook* (August 1922 – November-December 1923) was 'to bring Scottish literature into closer touch with current European tendencies in technique and ideation'. Although he and other Scottish post-translators have by no means confined themselves to 'current tendencies', one can surely say that in the last sixty-five years MacDiarmid's ambition has been richly fulfilled. So much is evident, we believe, from the translations printed here, but also, of course, from the great body of important original poetry written between 1922 and today. Scotland does indeed belong in Europe.

The relationship between the work of translation and the writing of original poetry was well stated by George Steiner in the introduction to his *Penguin Book of Modern Translation* (1966): 'Poetry translation plays a unique role inside the translator's own speech. It drives inward. Anyone translating a poem, or attempting to, is brought face to face, as by no other exercise, with the genius, bone-structure and limitations of his own native tongue'. The word 'limitations' is important here. Translation confronts the writer with something beyond his or her experience. Often the foreign text may lure one with its apparent familiarity or kinship. But it remains distant, different. And this is precisely why it is so important; it stretches the receiving tongue, forcing translator and reader into new efforts of imagination.

There have been periods, of course, when translators have sought to minimise this distance. 'To make Homer speak as if he had been born among us' was the ambition of some of his eighteenth-century translators. Since those days, we have doubtless become more aware of the differences between cultures, differences of time, place and language, and we are more likely to be suspicious of the abstract humanism which subjects all translated work to the tyrannical criterion of the 'good read'. What has remained with us, though, is the difficulty of finding a proper mean between faithfulness and beauty – assuming, as the sexist translation theorists of the seventeenth century did, that you can't have both. It is no doubt helpful to distinguish between imitation (to use Lowell's term) or adaptation and translation proper. But even within the latter domain, where we have tried to confine ourselves, there are constant choices to be made. Where Garioch's Belli has a Saint Christopher 'faur bigger nor a Glesca stevedore', Sydney Goodsir Smith's Corbière stays more firmly rooted in Brittany. In general, and naturally enough, it seems that translation into Scots pulls the foreign poem more strongly towards us, whereas English versions settle more easily in an unlocalised poetic space. Which works best will depend on the type of poem (not to speak of the skill of the translator), but it is hard to contest the superiority of Sydney Goodsir Smith's 'The Twal' or Edwin Morgan's Mayakovsky over their English rivals.

In purely quantitative terms, we have arrived (partly by chance) at a roughly equal balance between work in Scots and work in English. As far as the former is concerned, it will be evident that our translators have used many different versions of the language. On the one hand, there are those whose idiom is quite easily comprehensible to Scots and non-Scots alike (and this, contrary to some people's belief, is true of several of MacDiarmid's translations); at the other extreme, there is the Shetland Scots of W. J. Tait or the aureate style, studded with rare words or coinages, of some of the younger Scots poets. Since we hope that this anthology will find readers far beyond the borders of Scotland, we have provided a fairly full glossary at the end of the volume. Taken together with the *Concise Scots Dictionary*, edited by Mairi Robinson, this should make all the poems here accessible to all English-speaking readers.

In making this anthology, we have used only existing translations, for the most part published ones, and translations that seemed to us to work as poems. There could be no question therefore of attempting a balanced coverage of European poetry. Even so, it has proved possible to include translations from most of the principal languages of Europe, both ancient and modern. The main emphasis is on the modern period, but as befits a country with a strong tradition of education in the Classics, there are a fair number of poems from Latin and Greek. And in a country that has known its own recent Renaissance, it is natural that the Renaissance lyric of Italy, France and Spain should be well represented. As for the modern languages, Auld Alliance or no Auld Alliance, one notices the wealth of translations from the Italian and the Russian, both languages which are little studied in schools today and often regarded by educational planners as minor (or minority) languages. In the case of Russian, MacDiarmid's example (in the *Drunk Man*) has no doubt been fruitful, and a variety of political motivations have also played their part, but in any case it is heartening to see how Scottish poets (like poets in other countries) have shown themselves aware of the extraordinary richness of modern Russian poetry and looked to Russian culture for inspiration. The strength of the Italian connection (recently attested in Edinburgh by the Leopardi celebrations and the associated publication) is perhaps more difficult to account for, but it is a fact, and we would refer readers to R. D. S. Jack's *The Italian Influence on Scottish Literature* and *Scottish Literature's Debt to Italy* for a sympathetic discussion of the subject.

Scottish poets have shown themselves very open to the poetry of Europe; is the same true the other way round? Unlikely as its publication may be, it would certainly be interesting to see what a comparable anthology of Scottish poetry in the various European languages would look like. One suspects that with some honourable exceptions the tally would be slight, at any rate as far as the twentieth century is concerned. It is sobering to reflect that the most translated of Scottish poets was probably James Ossian-Macpherson, or perhaps Byron (and how many foreign readers regard him as a Scot?). But it has been well said that a culture can only be properly understood when it is seen from without as well as within, and we must hope that the image of Scotland conveyed by the poet-translators of other countries will contribute increasingly to this work of reciprocal self-definition.

For greater coherence, and because of limitations of space, we have confined ourselves to translations from the languages of continental Europe. This excludes, for example, the languages of Asia, but equally the languages of the British Isles. (The exception to this rule is Alexander Scott's 'Seaman's Sang', surely as successful a rendering as Pound's celebrated 'Seafarer'.) The most difficult question was that of Gaelic. After considerable reflection, we decided to include neither translations into Gaelic, nor translations from Gaelic into English or Scots. The former exclusion is to be explained partly by our own ignorance, but more generally we feel that the whole Gaelic issue is important enough to merit a separate publication rather than being given a small place here. It is good to know that such a volume is being prepared by Derick Thomson.

With few exceptions we have gone for whole poems rather than extracts, and are very glad to be able to print such masterpieces as

Valery's *Cimetière Marin* or Blok's *The Twelve*. In the case of short poems, it was sometimes tempting to publish more than one version of the same original. This can certainly be very interesting – one might cite for instance the recent Edinburgh University Press Leopardi, where translations of the same poem into the three languages of Scotland sit side by side. But since our aim was to show the range of European poetry that has been brought into Scotland by translators, it appeared wiser to resist the temptation. In some cases, where translations of the same poem seemed of roughly equal merit, we have chosen that of an author who was not already well represented here. This accords with our decision to bring in a fairly large number of translators rather than confining ourselves to the most well-known names, though of course such masters as Edwin Morgan and Alastair Mackie must command full representation. Beyond such considerations, like all anthologists, we have made a personal selection. George Steiner affirms that a good translation 'returns the reader to the original', while for T. S. Eliot the mark of a good translation is that a foreign writer is 'successfully done into the idiom of our own language and our own time'. We have had it as our aim to print in this book translations which meet this taxing double standard.

Prologue
Gavin Douglas

FROM THE LATIN OF VIRGIL

ENEADOS IV. XII

Heir followys of the famus Queyn Dydo
The fatale dynt of deth and mortale wo.

Bot now the hasty, egyr and wild Dydo,
Into hyr cruell purpos enragyt so,
The bludy eyn rollyng in hir hed,
Wan and ful paill for feir of the neir ded,
With chekis freklyt, and al of tychirris bysprent,
Quakyng throu dreid, ruschit furth, or scho wald stent,
Onto the innar wardis of hyr place,
As wod woman clam on the byng, allace!
And furth scho drew the Trojane swerd, fute hait,
A wapyn was never wrocht for syk a nate.
And sone as sche beheld Eneas clething,
And eik the bed bekend, a quhile wepyng,
Stude musyng in hir mynd, and syne, but baid,
Fel in the bed, and thir last wordis said:
'O sweit habyte, and lykand bed,' quod sche,
'So lang as God lyst suffir and destane,
Ressave my blude, and this sawle that on flocht is,
And me delyvir from thir hevy thochtis.
Thus lang I levyt have, and now is spent
The term of lyfe that forton heth me lent;
For now my gret gost undir erth mon go.
A richt fair cite have I beild alsso,
Myne awyn wark and wallys behald have I,
My spows wrokyn of my brothir ennemy,
Fra hym byreft hys tressour, and quyt hym weill.
Happy, allace! our happy, and ful of seyll,
Had I beyn, only gyf that never nane
At our cost had arryvit schip Trojane.'
And sayand this, hir mouth fast thristis sche
Doun in the bed: 'Onwrokyn sal we de?
De us behufis,' scho said, 'and quhou behald!'
And gan the scharp sword to hir breist uphald;
'Ya, thus, thus lykis us starve and to depart!'
And with that word, rave hir self to the hart.
'Now lat yon cruel Trojane swelly and se

This our fyre funerale from the deip see,
And of our deth turs with hym fra Cartage
Thys takyn of myscheif in hys vayage,'
Quod scho; and tharwith gan hir servandis behald
Hir fallyn and stekit on the irne cald,
The blude outbullyrand on the nakyt swerd,
Hir handis furthsprent. The clamour than and rerd
Went to the toppys of the large hallys;
The noys ran wild out our the cite wallis,
Smate all the town with lamentabil murnyng.
Of greting, gowlyng and wyfly womentyng
The ruffis dyd resound, bray and rayr,
Quhil huge bewalyng al fordynnyt the air –
Nane other wys than thocht takyn and doun bet
War al Cartage, and with ennemys ourset,
Or than thar natyve cite the town of Tyre,
And furyus flambe, kendillit and byrnand schyre,
Spredyng fra thak to thak, baith but and ben,
Als weil our templis as howsis of othir men.
Hir systir An, spreitles almaist for dreid,
Herand sa feirful confluens thyddir speid,
With nalys ryvand reuthfully hir face,
And smytand with hir nevis hir breist, allace!
Fast ruschis throu the myddis of the rowt,
And on the throwand, with mony sprauch and schout,
Callys by name: 'systir germane,' quod scho,
'Och! was this it thou fenyeit the to do?
Hes thou attempyt me with syk dissait?
This byng of treys, thir altaris and fyris hait,
Is this the thyng thai have onto me dycht?
Quhat sal I first compleyn, now dissolate wight?
O deir systir, quhen thou was reddy to de,
Ha! quhy hes thou sa far dyspysyt me
As to reffus thi systir with the to wend?
Thou suld have callyt me to the sammyn end,
That the ilk sorrow, the sammyn swerd, bath tway,
And the self hour, mycht have tane hyne away.
Thys funeral fyre with thir handis biggyt I,
And with my voce dyd on our goddis heir cry,
To that effect as, cruel, to be absent,
Thou beand thus sa duylfully heir schent!
Sistir, allace! with my counsell have I
The, and my self, and pepill of Sydony,
The heris all, and eik thi fayr cite,
Distroyt and ondoyn for ay,' quod sche.
'Fech hiddir sone the well watir lew warm,
To wesch hir woundis, and hald hir in myne arm;

Syne with my mowth at I may sowk, and se
Gyf spreit of lyve left in hir body be.'
This sayand, the hie byng ascendis onane,
And gan enbrays half ded hir systir germane,
Culyeand in hir bosum, and murnand ay,
And with hir wympil wipyt the blude away.
And scho agane, Dydo, the dedly queyn,
Pressyt fortil uplift hir hevy eyn,
Bot tharof falys; for the grysly wound
Deip in hir breist gapis wyde and onsound.
Thyrs scho hir self raxit up to rys;
Thrys on hir elbok lenys; and als feill sys
Scho fallys bakwart in the bed agane.
With eyn rollyng, and twynkland up ful fane,
Assays scho to spy the hevynnys lyght,
Syne murmouris, quhen scho tharof gat a sycht.
Almychty Juno havand reuth, by this,
Of hir lang sorow and tarysum ded, I wys,
Hir mayd Irys from the hevyn hes send
The throwand sawle to lowys, and mak ane end
Of al the juncturis and lethis of his cors;
Becaus that nothir of fatis throu the fors
Nor yit by natural ded peryschit sche,
Bot fey in hasty furour emflambyt hie
Befor hir day had hir self spilt,
Or that Proserpyne the yallow haris gilt
From hir fortop byreft, or dubbyt hir hed
Onto the Stygian hellis flude of ded.
Tharfor dewy Iris throu the hevyn
With hir safron weyngis flaw ful evin,
Drawand, quhar scho went, forgane the son cleir,
A thousand cullouris of divers hewys seir,
And abufe Dydoys hed arest kan:
'I am commandyt,' said scho, 'and I man
Omdo this hayr, to Pluto consecrate,
And lowis thi sawle out of this mortale stait.'
Thys sayand, with rycht hand hes scho hynt
The hair, and cuttis in twa, or that scho stynt;
And tharwithall the natural heyt outquent,
And, with a puft of aynd, the lyfe furthwent.

*Heir endys the ferd buke of Eneados
and begynnys the proloug of the fyft*

3

Alexander Gray

FROM THE GERMAN OF HEINRICH HEINE

SONGS

1

The starns have stood still for ages,
Far up in the lift sae hie;
They roun to themsels sae sadly
O' a love that can never dee.

They speak to ilk ither a language,
Sae bonny and couthy and bien;
But nane o' the college callants
Can tell what the laigh words mean.

But I ken weel what they're sayin',
And I'll forget it nae mair.
My schule-book was Bettie's blue een
And the glint o' her gowden hair.

2

You say you dinna lo'e me, Jean?
That winna gar me dee.
Just let me see your bonny een,
And wha sae blithe as me?

I hear your bonny reid lips say
You hate me, lass! O fie!
Just let me kiss them nicht and day—
And what the deil care I?

3

Nae plaint I'll mak, although my hert should brak,
My love for ever tint, nae plaint I'll mak.
What though you glint wi' silks and diamonds bricht.
Nae glint o' licht'll reach your hert's mirk nicht.

Lang syne I kent it. In a dream I saw
Nicht, cauld and blae, upon your puir hert fa'.
I saw your hert, wi' channerin' neddars there;
I saw you maun be wae for evermair.

4

4

Upon your bonny cheeks, lass,
The summer's roses sleep.
Upon your saikless young hert
The winter's snaw lies deep.

I doot, my bonny lassie,
But that'll sune gae 'wa',
The summer will won in your hert, love,
Your cheeks will be white as the snaw.

5

The auld sangs soored and cankered,
Ill dreams that keep me fleyed—
Let's get a michty coffin,
And stow them a' inside.

There's muckle I maun lay there,
Though what I daurna tell.
The coffin maun be bigger
Than St. Andrews' auld draw-well.

And bring a bier, weel-timmered,
O' brods baith lang and wide:
Needs be they maun be langer
Than the auld brig ower the Clyde.

And bring me twal' great giants,
A' men o'muckle worth—
As strang as William Wallace
That looks across the Forth.

And they maun tak the coffin
And sink it in the wave,
For sic a michty coffin
Maun hae a michty grave.

D'ye ken what wey the coffin
Maun be sae grite and strang?
It's my love I mean to lay there,
And the dule I've tholed sae lang.

6

The nicht's deid still; there's no a soon'.
In this hoose dwalt the lass I lo'ed.
It's lang, lang sin' she quat the toon,
But aye the hoose stands whaur it stude.

A callant stands and gowps abune;
He seems to dree the rage o' Hell.
It gars me grue when by the mune
I see nane ither than mysel'.

You ill-daein' wraith, gae hod your face.
What gars you geck at a' the pein
That ance I tholed upon this place
Sae money a nicht in auld lang syne?

7

I glowered upon her picture;
Auld dreams cam back ance mair;
I thocht life cam rekindlin'
Her face as I stude there.

A bonny smile cam playin'
Aboot her rosy mou';
Her een shone through her greetin'
Like violets weet wi' dew.

My hert cam near to brakin';
I cudna stop my tears.
Ach lass, and hae I tint you
Through a' the weary years?

8

It's a coorse, coorse nicht and it's rainin';
There's an onding o' snaw forbye.
I sit by the winnock glowerin'
At the bowsterous, mirky sky.

I see a licht sheenin' its lanesome;
It slowly comes doon the street.
A mither bearin' a lantern.
Gaes draiglin' through the weet.

The body has coft some butter
And sugar and eggs and meal.
She's ettin' to be at the bakin',
For her lassie's at hame no weel.

She leans her heid on the bowster,
And drowsily blinks at the licht.
Her hair that hings roond her shouthers
Sheens bonny and gowden and bricht.

9

There were three kings cam frae the East;
They spiered in ilka clachan:
"O, which is the wey to Bethlehem,
My bairns, sae bonnily lachin'?"

O neither young nor auld could tell;
They trailed till their feet were weary.
They followed a bonny gowden starn,
That shone in the lift sae cheery.

The starn stude ower the ale-hoose byre
Whaur the stable gear was hingin'.
The owsen mooed, the bairnie grat,
The kings begoud their singin'.

10

O, you're braw wi' your pearls and your diamonds,
    You've rowth o' a' thing, you may say;
And there's nane has got bonnier een, Kate:
    'Od, lassie, what mair wad you hae?

I've written a hantle o' verses,
    That'll live till the Hendmost Day;
And they're a' in praise o' your een, Kate:
    'Od, lassie, what mair wad you hae?

Your een, sae blue and sae bonny,
    Have plagued me till I am fey.
'Deed, I hardly think I can live, Kate:
    'Od, lassie, what mair wad you hae?

Hugh MacDiarmid

FROM THE DUTCH OF PIETER CORNELISZOON HOOFT

PEACE

This warl', wi'ts muckle mount'ins, twined wi' streams;
Speckled wi' cities ringed aboot wi' to'ers;
Wha's face wi' hill an' lauchin' valley gleams,
Wha's darksome wuds are sawn wi' canny flo'ers;
The birds; an' gangrel beasts aneath the mune;
An' even the puir pridefu' stock o' man
Are a' alike haud'n in by luve, an' sune
Withouten love 'ud lapse frae nature's plan.

I' nowt but luve earth's cities can be reared
An' ha'e guid growth an' flourish: strife's their daith.
Thro' civil wars they pech wi' waesome braith.
Dissension gnaws the roots o' ony State:
I' luve alane the seeds o' joy can braird,
An' peace at hame mak's little countries great.

FROM THE RUSSIAN OF AFANASY FET

THE AERIAL CITY

At the peep o day in the lift forgether
    Bonnie cloods like a steepled toun,
Wi mony a dome like a bubble o gowd
    And white roofs and white waas blinterin doun.

O yon is my ain white city –
    Or I cam to the earth I bade there!
Abune the derk warld quhile it sleeps
    In the reid lift skinklan fair.

But it hauds awa to the North,
    Sails saftly, saftly, and high –
And a voice is fain that I'd join it –
    But gies me nae wings to try.

8

FROM THE GERMAN OF STEFAN GEORGE

Ye kenna wha I am—but this is fac'.
I ha'ena yet by ony word or ac'
Made mysel' human . . . an' sune I maun tak'
Anither guise to ony I've yet ta'en
I'll cheenge: an' yet my ain true sel' I'll hain,
Tine only what ye ken as me. I' vain
Ye'll seek to haud me, an' ye needna murn,
For to a form ye canna ken I'll turn
'Twixt ae braith an' the neist: an' whan I'm gane
Ye'll ha'e o' me what ye ha'e o' a'
My kindred since licht on the erth 'good da' –
The braith that gi'es ye courage, an' the fain
Wild kiss that aye into your saul maun burn.

FROM THE RUSSIAN OF ZINAIDA HIPPIUS

A shameless thing, for ilka vileness able,
It is deid grey as dust, the dust o' a man.
I perish o' a nearness I canna win awa' frae,
Its deidly coils aboot my buik are thrawn.

A shaggy poulp, embracin' me and stingin',
And as a serpent cauld agen' my hert,
Its scales are poisoned shafts that jag me to the quick
– And waur than them's my scunners' feerfu' smert!

O that its prickles were a knife indeed,
But it is thowless, flabby, dowf, and numb.
Sae sluggishly it drains my benmaist life
A dozent dragon, dreidfu', deef, and dumb.

In mum obscurity it twines its obstinate rings
And hings caressin'ly, its purpose whole;
And this deid thing, whale-white obscenity,
This horror that I writhe in – is my soul!

FROM THE GERMAN OF RAINER MARIA RILKE

REQUIEM FOR A WOMAN

I have been frequently astonished, letting go
My dead at last, to see them so at home
In death, so unexpectedly at rights,
So in their element that in a trice
'Twas ill to fathom they had ever lived. . . .
You only, you come back, and seem to try
To come in touch with something that will ring
Out suddenly, and show that you are here. . . .
O rob me not of what I've hardly learnt,
For I am right and you are wrong if still
You covet anything of so-called life.
We change all this, and see there's nothing here
In the clear light of our perfected selves.

I had more faith in you, and it confounds
All my ideas to find you here again,
You who changed most abysmally of all.
Not that your death is still incredible
(Although the manner of it tore apart
All we had been from aught we since could be
And made it difficult for us to find
Ourselves again). The trouble is that you
Were terrified to die, and keep your fear
Where fear is out of question, and so lose
A bit of your eternity, and lapse
Back here where nothing is as yet itself
– That broken, merged for the first time in the All,
You cannot see as even here you could
Life's upward irreversible way, and fall
By the dead weight of grievance from the spheres
To which you now belong to this poor past.
– *That* wakes me often like a thief at night.

Would I could think that you came sportively,
Because you are too certain of yourself,
O'erspilling your abundance, like a child
Going careless where grown folks must needs have care.
But ah! You ask for something. In my bones
That fact goes back and forward like a saw.
You ask for something. Though you were a dream
Tormenting me, pursuing me at nights,
When I retreat into my lungs and bowels
And the last poorest chamber of my heart,
E'en that were easier borne. . . . What do you ask?

What can I do for you? Is something, left
Behind you inadvertently, crying
Incessantly to find where you have gone
And vainly craving to be after you?
Where is it? Must I seek it in some part
Of life you never knew you had at all –
And failed to reckon with before you died?
Then I'll go there at once, and watch the ways
Of women about the doors and with their young,
Converse with all and sundry, and secure
An audience of the King, suborn the priests
To let me enter their holy places – yea,
And above all I will, when I've learned much,
Look simply at the animals until
An essence from them imperceptibly
Glides into me – stand in their eyes awhile
And witness how they put me out again
Gently, incuriously, and unjudged.

I'll get the gardeners to name their flowers
That in what I remember I may bring
Some faint suggestions of their myriad scents;
And fruits – I'll buy fruits till that country's like
Our old idea of what Heaven would be.

Full fruits! Ah, these you understood, set them
On plates before you, counterbalancing
Their weights with colours; and like fruits you saw
Women and children driven hither from within
Into their lives, and naked bore yourself
Fruit-like at last before the mirror here
Looking at yourself till like a pool your look
Closed over you, insubstantialised
(And no more saying: "This am I, no that is")
In those pure depths from which it had no wish
That you should ever re-emerge. Blessed!

Thus had I kept you, as you steeped yourself
Deep in the mirror. Why come differently?
What to recant? To tell me what? Is there
A sacrificial weight in amber beads
A visual recollection fails to show?   .
My memory cannot tell the purport now
Of looks so urgent and discharactered,
Or why your body's graces all appear
Like lines of destiny on an outheld palm.

11

Come to the candle. I don't fear the dead.
If they are to be seen my eyes will see
Them naturally enough. Come hither then.
See this cut rose. The light's as shy of it
As 'tis of you. It, too, need not be here,
But if't had stayed outside, unmixed with me,
It would have kept on growing and ere this
Have fallen apart – whereas it lingers here;
And yet – what is my consciousness to it?

Do not be frightened if I understand,
(Ah, there! It comes to me) for I must know
Even though the knowledge kills. I know you're here.
Even as a blind man fumbles round a thing
I feel your plight and have no name for it.
Let us lament together – the broken mirror
And you found naked in your hiding place.

Can you still weep? You cannot. All your tears
Contributed to ripen you and sent
The saps within you mounting in a life
That climbed and circled – to that height from which
Your fate reclaimed you, taking bit by bit
And daily more, till nothing but the core
Was left, full of the green seeds of your death;
And these you tasted in your hunger too
And found an after-sweetness in your mouth.

From this self-sacrifice your life returned
All trembling and mistrustful to its tasks.
How strange your most familiar organs seemed
(All save that one, exigent and estranged)
To your blood refluent from that secret source
Whether you had to drive it, make it eat,
Again and yet again, the while it looked,
The ingrate thing, as though you poisoned it.
You forced it finally – and lo! it ran
Too fast, too fast, it ran. You sought to cry:
"Whoa there! You're far enough. Too far for me
To herd you back" – but suddenly you knew
'Twas gone too far indeed, beyond recall.
The time to drive it back would come no more
Like a recurrent illness. You were free.
How short your life was, put against the hours
You sat surrendering all you might have been
To that blind germ of destiny again.

12

O tragic task! O task beyond all power!
How day by day you undid all you'd grown,
Made yourself down to other ends and still
Had courage to be proud of doing it well,
And then you looked for your reward at last
As children do when they take medicine
But you'd to do your own rewarding too
You were too far away from us even then.
No one could think of anything to please.
You knew it, and sat up in childbed there
And from the mirror that was you received
Your own self back, eager as a woman is
Dressing for visitors and doing her hair.

And so you died, as other women died
Before you in that cosy home, the death
Of women lying-in, who'd close themselves
Again, and only be themselves, but ah!
Cannot because the darkness enters in
And will not be denied – the darkness that
Women give birth to with – the outer dark.

Surely the keening women should have keened
In truth – women who weep for pay and whine
The whole night through, if they are paid enough,
When there's no other sound. Customs, hither.
We need more customs. Let us show our grief.
We acquiesce too readily – and so
You, dead, come back that you and I may mourn
Your death more adequately. Hear me then.
Fain would I throw my voice as 'twere a cloth
Over your remains, and have all I am
Torn into rags for ever, were mourning all.
Beyond all lamentation I accuse –
Not him who drew you back out of yourself
(I do not know him – he is all mankind)
But I impeach the world in him the Man.

If my life holds a state of having been
A child I can't recall – the purest state
Of being a child my earliest childhood knew,
I do not want to know it – I want to make
An angel of it without seeing it
And send it into the very front rank

Of shouting angels who remember God.
The agony has lasted far too long.
It is beyond us – this anachronism
Of false love spawning out of habit,
And claiming as its rights the wrongs it does.
Where is the man who has the right to own
What only snatches itself up at nights
Blissfully as a child might snatch a ball?

Are you still here, unseen? You knew as much
Of all this and might have had so much,
Open for everything, like a dawning day.
Women can suffer. To love's to be alone.
Poets know love's a readiness to change.
You were both woman and poet, and both form part
Of what our memories distort as you.
You grew so homely, taking in your looks
Like flags the morning after a fête – and all
You wanted was a long day's work, but ah!
The work was never done – is not done yet!

If you're still here – if in this darkness there's
A place in which your spirit hovers still
About the tired sounds of my lonely voice
Hear me, help me, for see we disappear,
Not knowing when, into anything beyond our thought
Even as a landsman's eyesight fails to hold
The Deity on the shoulders of a ship,
When its own lightness lifts it suddenly
Up and away into the bright sea wind. . . .

FROM THE RUSSIAN OF ALEXANDER BLOK

THE STRANGER

At darknin' hings abune the howff
A weet and wild and eisenin' air.
Spring's spirit wi' its waesome sough
Rules owre the drucken stramash there.

And heich abune the vennel's pokiness,
Whaur a' the white-weshed cottons lie,
The Inn's sign blinters in the mochiness,
And lood and shrill the bairnies cry.

The hauflins 'yont the burgh boonds
Gang ilka nicht, and a' the same,
Their bonnets cocked; their bluid that stounds
Is playin' at a fine auld game.

And on the lochan there, hauf-herted
Wee screams and creakin' oar-locks soon',
And in the lift, heich, hauf-averted,
The mune looks owre the yirdly roon'.

And ilka evenin', derf and serious
(Jean ettles nocht o' this, puir lass),
In liquor, raw yet still mysterious,
A'e freend's aye mirrored in my glass.

Ahint the sheenin' coonter gruff
Thrang barmen ding the tumblers doun;
"In vino veritas" cry rough
And reid-een'd fules that in it droon.

But ilka evenin' fey and fremt
(Is it a dream nae wauk'nin' proves?)
As to a trystin'-place undreamt,
A silken leddy darkly moves.

Slow gangs she by the drunken anes,
And lanely by the winnock sits;
Frae'r robes, atour the sunken anes,
A rooky dwamin' perfume flits.

Her gleamin' silks, the taperin'
O' her ringed fingers, and her feathers
Move dimly like a dream wi'in,
While endless faith aboot them gethers.

I seek, in this captivity,
To pierce the veils that darklin' fa'
– See white clints slidin' to the sea,
And hear the horns o' Elfland blaw.

15

I ha'e dark secrets' turns and twists,
A sun is gi'en to me to haud,
The whisky in my bluid insists,
And spiers my benmaist history, lad.

And owre my brain the flitterin'
O' the dim feathers gang aince mair,
And, faddomless, the dark blue glitterin'
O' twa een in the ocean there.

My soul stores up this wealth unspent,
The key is safe and nane's but mine.
You're richt, auld drunk impenitent,
I ken it tae – the truth's in wine!

FROM THE ITALIAN OF GIUSEPPE UNGARETTI

1

CONTRITE

I gang prowlin' roon'
My sheep's body
Wi' the hunger o' a wolf.

I am like
A wallowin' barge
On a tumultuous ocean.

2

WEEP AND WAIL NO MORE

Stop killin' the deid. Gi'e owre
Your weepin' and wailin'. You maun keep quiet
If you want to hear them still
And no' blur their image in your mind.

For they've only a faint wee whisperin' voice
Makin' nae mair noise ava'
Than the growin' o' the grass
That flourishes whaur naebody walks.

16

FROM THE GERMAN OF RUDOLF LEONHARD

THE DEAD LIEBKNECHT

His corpse owre a' the city lies
In ilka square and ilka street
His spilt bluid floods the vera skies
And nae hoose but is darkened wi't.

The factory horns begin to blaw
Thro' a' the city, blare on blare,
The lowsin' time o' workers a',
Like emmits skailin' everywhere.

And wi' his white teeth shinin' yet
The corpse lies smilin' underfit.

William Soutar

DO NOT TOUCH

Haud aff, haud aff, the pent is weet:
The saul nor fash'd the least:
Memory kythes in the glimmerin e'e;
In hands, and lips, and breist.

O! far yont a' oor guid or ill,
For this you were sae dear;
That the white licht, noo greyly gaen,
In you was aye mair clear.

And yet, and yet, I ken my gloom
Will grow, because o' you,
Whiter nor lamplicht, nor the white
Bandage about your broo.

FROM THE RUSSIAN OF SERGEI YESENIN

POEM

The fower thackit wa's I was born in
Are stanes on a brae:
And here in the yowtherin vennels
I am weirded to dee.

What thocht hae I noo o' gae'n back there
Whaur the fields are forforn;
And the lanely whaup cries owre a muirland
That micht hae been corn.

Yet I lo'e this auld, scowtherie city;
A hell o' a toun;
The lamplicht abüne the black water
That slooms by wi' sma' soun'.

And it's then, whan awa owre the garrets
The müne breels alang,
That I lowch to the howff whaur sae aften
I've gaen – and will gang.

18

And a' through the nicht, wi' its stramash,
Sculdudry and sin,
I reel aff my sangs to the trollops
And shove round the gin;

Or the hert stounds sae loud in my breist,
This is a' I can cry:
I am lost, you are lost, we are a' lost,
And ken na the wey.

The fower thackit wa's I was born in
Are stanes on a brae:
And here in the yowtherin vennels
I am weirded to dee.

William Montgomerie

FROM THE ANONYMOUS GERMAN

RHYMES FROM DES KNABEN WUNDERHORN

1

Quivit quaevit
the deuks aw gang barefit
the geese's feet are wat
Whit dae the wee hens think o' that?

An whan I cam tae the Irish Sea
I fund three men an mair than three
the tane had naething ava
the tither had naething at aw
an the third had nocht

They coft a hapny bap
an a hunnerwecht o gusty cheese
an gaed wi't tae the Irish Sea

An whan they cam tae the Irish Sea
than they cam tae a toom toom land
aw banes an sand
an they cam tae a paper kirk
an a sandstane meenister coopit
in a wee ledder poopit
wha cried

"We hae sinned the day
gin God gie us life we'll aye dae sae"

An the three sisters o Lazarus
Catrina Sybil Stey still
grat bitterly
an the cock crawed buttermulk

2

The Scots Greys ride
sabres by their side

Cut the mannie's ear aff!
Na jist cut it near aff!

Lea a wee bit o his lug
an next time we'll ken the dog

20

FROM THE GERMAN OF RAINER MARIA RILKE

SOLEMN HOUR

Wha noo greets onywhaur i the warld
withoot cause greets i the warld
  greets ower me

What noo lauchs onywhaur i the nicht
withoot cause lauchs i the nicht
  lauchs me oot

Wha noo gaes onygate i the warld
withoot cause gaes i the warld
  gaes tae me

Wha noo dees onywhaur i the warld
withoot cause dees i the warld
  luiks at me

J. K. Annand

FROM THE ANONYMOUS MEDIEVAL LATIN

PLANGIT NONNA

A nun is sabbin sairly
She'd deave ye wi her granes
As girnin, greetin rarely
She says ontil her friends:
    "Wae's me!
Nocht could e'er be waur
    Nor sic a life.
I'd raither be a hure
    Or randy wife.

I jow the haly bell,
O psalms I tell my stent.
I'm waukent in my cell
Wi radgie dreams fair spent
    (Wae's me)
To nichtlang vigil keep
    Och sae sweirly,
When wi a man I'd sleep
    Baith late and early."

FROM THE FRENCH OF PIERRE DE RONSARD

ELEGY ON THE DEPAIRTURE
O MARY QUEEN O SCOTS ON HER
RETOUR TIL HER KINRICK O SCOTLAND

Like a braw meedow rypit o its flouers
Like a pentin deprivit o its colours
Like the lift when it has tint its stars,
The sea, its waters; the ship, sails and spars,
Like a field laid bare when they've gethert the corn
Or a wuid whase leafy green mantle is shorn,
Or a ring that has tint its precious stane,
Juist sae a doilsome France sall tine
Her ornament and beauty bricht,
Her flouer, her colour, and her licht.

Dour Fortune, traitorous and felloun,
Truly the dochter o a lion,
Your tiger claws can gar us smert
I dout that ye maun want a hert
Sicwyse to use our bonnie Queen.

When she was but a breist-fed wean
Ye weirdit her to dule and wae
When on her minnie's lap she lay
And garred her mither bield her in
A place the English wadna fin'.
Fresh frae the cradle, still a bairn
Ye set her on a ship, sea-farin
Forsakin her mither, her land o birth
And croun, to dwall on France's yirth.
'Twas then ye had a cheynge o hert
Ettlin to play a gentler pairt
(A maist unsiccar gait ye've trod)
Ye took thon orphan frae abroad
And had her on our Dauphin merrit
That wad the croun o France inherit.
Syne, hertless Fortune, when ye fand
She had great honour in the land
Ye killed her man, aged but saxteen,
As in a gairden may be seen
A lily die when teemin rain
Cleaves its wearie powe in twain
Or as in simmer heat the rose
By gloamin time nae langer glows,
Ilk coloured petal's blude is shed
And leaf by leaf faas withered.

His braw young wife, wi grief gane gyte
Eftir his daith fand nae delyte
And like, in the wuid, the wedowed doo
That's tint her mate sae leal and true
And never will seek anither sire
Sin daith has murthert her desire
She sits in leafy glade nae mair,
Nae mair her voice sings sweet and clear,
In dern far ben the wuid she bides
And til the trees her dule confides.
There she kythes in grief and pain
And on a weazand trunk maks maen.

23

Fortune, ye wrocht owre muckle skaith
Devisin sic a piteous daith;
Ye needna brocht to her estait
A rowth o wrangs and war and hate
And gart her kinrick be invadit
Afore it was by sects dividit.

Gif the fury o your hands, sae cruel,
Has sic pouer owre things beautiful,
Gif aa the virtue, pitie, gudeness,
Douceness melled intil demureness,
Sanctlike weys and puritie
Didna resist your cruel envie,
Let's hope in our humanitie,
Nocht waur arise nor vanitie.
Hevin doesna bliss us aye wi smiles
But thunders doun its anger whiles
Juist as ye mar the ploys and sport
O the braw leddies o the court;
They that soud hae the pride and pouer
Canna withstand that dreid dolour.
Nor will ye, Fortune, be content
Wi ploys and pliskies to torment,
Ye'd reive us o our noble dame.
Ye pit the vera starns to shame
To tak this aipple o our ee
And cast her on the stormy sea.
Wad cliff rax owre to cliff in band
And gar the sea become dry land
And stop the ship that wad convoy
Our pride, our comfort, and our joy,
This honorit beauty o our time
Beluvit in palace and humble hame.

Och, Scotland, I could wish that ye
To wander hyne awa were free,
Your anchor tows that haud sae strang,
Wad ye could brek them lowse and gang
Randily vaigin, raff and ree
Like mallie skimmin owre the sea
To vanish frae our ken afore
The tardy ship can win your shore
Sae that ye never sall sustein
Within her realm your bonnie Queen.
Syne sall she, seekin ye in vain
Mak her retour to France again
To bide in her duchy o Touraine.

Frae rowth o sangs I'll nocht refrain
But in my verses praise her lang
And like a swan I'll die in sang.
Her beauty than sall be my theme
Her daithless virtues sing supreme
Where nou, on viewin her depairt
I sing o nocht but dule and smert.

Come, Elegie, in garment black,
On heichest craig your stance to tak,
Flie hyne awa frae haunts o men
Seek forests far ayont their ken
Amang the waters sing your plaint
Tell to the winds I lately tint
A Maistress and a pearl o price
Patron o virtuous men and wyce.
Divine rare Marguerite, poets' joy
Nou merrit and in far Savoy
– And nou I've a tint a Queen sae rare
My verse sall weep for evermair.

FROM THE GERMAN OF GERRIT ENGELKE

TO DAITH

Spare me a wee while, Daith,
The fire o youtheid's in my braith
My lowsin-time is still afar
The future aye is rowed in haar
　　Sae spare me yet, oh Daith.

But come back later, Daith,
When, life sair dune, nae langer laith,
Wi my forfochen hert aa spent,
The warld will tak o me nae tent.
　　Come then, and tak me, Daith.

Robert Garioch

FROM THE GREEK OF HESIOD

ANATOMY OF WINTER

In Februar come foul days, flee them gin ye may,
wi their felloun frosts, days that wad flype a nowt,
what Boreas blaws owre Thrace, whaur they breed the horses,
and brulyies the braid sea, and garrs it blawp;
and the winterous warld and the woddis warsle aathegither.
Monie a michty aik-tree and muckle-heidit pine
it dings til the dirt, our genetrice; wi the dunt as it faas
on the glens and the gowls atween the hills, syne the hale forest girns.
It garrs the bestial grue; their tails in the grooves
of their hurdies are steikit weill hame. The hairy yins and aa,
wi coats of guid cleidin, it cuts richt throu them;
the weill-happit hide of an ox, that duisnae haud out the cauld.
And it gangs throu a gait's lang hair. But gimmers and yowes
wi fouth of fleece, the wund flegs them nocht,
tho it bends an auld man's back, bow'd like a wheel.
And it canna skaith the saft skin of a young lass
that bienlie bides at hame, beside her dear mither,
onwittand as yet the ongauns of maist aureat Aphrodite.
But she wesches weill her flesch, and wycelie anoints it
wi ulyie of the best olives, syne beddis ben the hous.
The Baneless Yin bites his fuit, tholan bad weather –
wi nae heat frae hearth-stane, the hous is dowie.
The sun sairs him nocht to seek his food outbye;
he swees owre the cities of swart savage folk
but frae his saitt celestial is sweirt to shine on the Greeks.
Syne the hirsel of hornit kye, and their hornless baists,
wend throu the wuids: wearily they grind their teeth,
thirlit in aefald thocht, to find in their need
a bield to bide in, or a boss cave.
Trauchlit in siccan times, they traivel about
like luittard loons that limp on three legs
wi lumbago in the lunyie, aye luikan on the grund;
they hirple hobland about, hap-shackellit they seem;
hainan their bodies' heat, haud awa frae the white snaw-wreaths.
Sae pit on, I pray ye, as protection for yir flesch,
a saft goun and a sark streetchan to yir feet;
let it be woven wi muckle weft til a puckle warp,
that the hairs of yir bodie may be at rest, no birssy wi the cauld. . . .
Mak yirsel a kid-skin cape to keep out the rain,
and a felt hat wi laced lappits, syne yir lugs will be dry;
for yir neb will be nithert whan the nor-wund blaws;

at day-daw the hairst-nourissand haar, frae the hevin of sterns,
blankets the braid yird, bieldan the parks of the rich.
The haar soukit in steam frae ever-bounteous stremis
is blawn heich abuin the yird by blaisters of wund.
At dirknin it whiles draws to rain; whiles the blast's deray
is ruggan at thwankan cluddis thruschit by Thracian Boreas.

FROM THE ROMAN OF GIUSEPPE BELLI

SONNETS

1

CAIN

Cain, dominie, I'll no speak up fir him,
fir I ken mair nor ye dae anent Cain:
wine, aince in a while, that's aa I'm sayin,
can cheenge a man and mak his conscience dim.

I ken, to teer yir brither limb frae limb,
or pash his heid in wi a muckle stane,
is a gey keillie-mainnert wey of daein,
a guffie bit of wark, jist sae, maist grim.

But, seein Gode wes aye crabbit and dour
whan he brocht neeps, honey and sunflure-seed,
tho Abel's milk and yowes were Gode's plesure,

til a man like hiz-yins, made of flesh and bleed,
it wes eneuch to make his bile turn sour:
and sae, my freend, slash, slash, whan he saw reid.

2

JUDGMENT DAY

Fowre muckle angels wi their trumpets, stalkin
till the fowre airts, sall aipen the inspection;
they'll gie a blaw, and bawl, ilk to his section,
in their huge voices: "Come, aa yese, be wauken."

27

Syne sall crawl furth a ragment, a haill cleckin
of skeletons yerkt out fir resurrection
to tak again their ain human complexion,
like choukies gaitheran roun a hen that's clockan.

And thon hen sall be Gode the blissit Faither;
he'll pairt the indwellars of mirk and licht,
tane doun the cellar, to the ruiff the tither.

Last sall come angels, swarms of them, in flicht,
and, like us gaean to bed without a swither,
they will blaw out the caunnles, and guid-nicht.

3

THE PAIP

Gode wants the Paip unmairret, for fear he'd mak
wee paipikies pop up and see the licht:
syne aa the cardinals, puir craturs, micht
be left tuim-neive'd, naething for them to tak.

But, for aa that, the Paip can tag-up slack
knots as he likes, or lowse thaim that are ticht,
mak sancts of hiz, or hide us frae Christ's sicht,
and bash out blinlans wi ane michtie whack.

Aside this binding and unbinding trock,
he carries two keys firtae tell the story
that this yin aipens, thon yin steiks, the shop.

And that gret muckle haggis-shapit toorie
means he's the heid-yin, wadnae gie a dock,
and rules the yird, hevin and purgatory.

4

THE GUID FAIMLY

Faither wins hame, my grannie leaves her wheel,
puir sowl, gies owre her spinning for the nicht;
she lays the buird, blaws her wee coal alicht,
and we sit-in to sup our puckle kail.

We mak oursels an omelet, aince in a while,
gey thin, sae's ye can fairly see the licht
throu it, jist like it wes a lug: aa richt,
we chaw a puckle nuts, and that's our meal.

While Faither and mysel and Clementine
bide on, she clears the buird, gaes aff and redds
the kitchie, and we drink a drappie wine.

The wee carafe timmit doun til the dregs,
a wee strone, a hailmary said, and syne,
lither and lown, we sclimm intill our beds.

5

THE REMINDER

D'ye mind of thon auldfarrant-leukan priest
that learnt folk in their ain houses, him
wi twa white linen bands aboot his kist,
a muckle goun of some coorse kinna scrim?

that stuid amang the heid-stanes, his lang, thin
shanks like twa parritch-spirtles, niver missed
a yirdin, him that gaed til the Sun Inn
fir denner, and wad pey a hauf-croun, jist!

Aweill, the ither day, they fand him deid
and hingit, wi a raip about his throat
tied til the crucifix-heuk abuin his bed.

And this wee ploy of his meant sic a lot
to him, to keep the maitter in his heid,
he'd even tied his hankie in a knot.

6

THE RULERS OF THE AULD WARLD

Yince on a time there wes a King, wha sat
screivan this edict in his palace-haa
til aa his fowk: "Vassals, I tell ye flat
that I am I, and you are bugger-aa.

I mak richt wrang, wrang richt, my word is law:
I can sell yese, sae muckle fir the lot:
If I hing yese, ye're no ill-yaised ava,
ye rent yir lives and gear frae me, that's that.

Whasae bides in this warld, bot the title
either of Paip, or Emperor, or King,
sall niver mell in oniething that's vital."

The heidsman tuke this edict roun in sicht
of aa the fowk, speiran anent this thing,
and they aa said til him: *That's richt, that's richt.*

7

THE WEE THIEF'S MITHER

Eh, whit's he nickit oniewey?! a heap
of junk, fowre umberellies, a watch or twa,
hankies. Whit a cufuffle, eftir aa,
as if he'd killt the Monarch of the Deep.

Puir sowl, he's tawrrie-fingert; can ye caa
the thieves brithers nae mair, nor staund their keep?!
Gin Walter is a wolf, whaur are the sheep?
There's nane bit Gode hes naethin wrang ava.

Plenty fowk, Excellency, that git on fine,
steal hunners mair nor him, and niver falter,
and they win reverence, and dine, and wine.

I've aye gien this advice til him: Son Walter,
lift hauf a million; fir the churches, syne,
ye'll be a sanct, wi lilies on yer altar.

8

THE LIFE OF MAN

Nine months in the stink, syne rowed-up, dosed wi dill,
mang kisses, milk, greitan and curly locks,
harnessed, happit in babby-clouts and frocks,
in a bairn-fank pentit wi Jack and Jill.

And syne stairts aa the torment of the schuil,
the A.B.C. and chulblains, pawmies, knocks,
the cackie doun the hole, a puckle poax,
rush-fever, measles or some ither ill.

Syne lairnin hou to fast and mak a levin,
the rent, the government, the presoun cell,
hospital, dyvourie, mockage and grieving,

the simmer suin, the winter snaw and hail. . . .
And at the feenish o't, Gode bliss us, even
eftir aa thon, comes daith and, lastly, hell.

9

SANCT CHRISTOPHER II

Sanct Christopher's a muckle sanct and strang,
faur bigger nor a Glesca stevedore,
wha, owre some river, barefuit, on his lang
shanks, yuistae cairry folk frae shore to shore.

Maybe thon river he wad aye owregang
wes a smaa burn, or dub left frae a shouer;
that's aa I ken about it, richt or wrang;
I tell ye jist whit I wes tellt afore.

Yae day he cairried a wee boy. Nae suiner
did he wyde in, but he wes near owreharl'd;
muckle Sanct Christopher begood to founder.

"By Christ! whit kinna trick is this?" he snarled.
"Son, ye're an aafie wecht, a richt wee wunner!
whit's this I hae upon my back; the Warld?"

10

NOAH'S ARK

Elephants, wolves, Scotch terriers and chows,
chihuahuas, cuddies, wallabies and bears,
stallions, cats, choukies, birds, hogs, moussies, hares,
foxes; flees, grumphies, lions, cous and yowes.

Melon-rinds, birdseed, vermicelli, maize,
braxy, haill ricks of hey, bran, clover, banes,
bere-water drinks for horses, minced ox-hairts,
kebbucks and crowdie – that's twa kinds of cheese.

Aa thae – and there wes faur mair whaur they cam frae
that I missed out – gaed intil Noah's Ark.
Bieldit by Gode, aa round the warld to Wamphray

and back, ae year and mair, soumit their bark!
But hou did he get on wi thon clanjamphrie?
Best speir, my friens, at the guid Patriarch.

31

11

DEID

Dae ye no ken wha passed awa yestreen?
My cuddy, Repiscitto, met his fate;
puir beastie, that wes aye sae douce and quate
his back micht hae been ridden by a queen.

I'd hardly cam out frae the miller's yett
wi sacks o flour, hou monie? – juist a wheen
hunnerwechts or sae, he'd faaen doun thirteen
times as it wes; he tummilt ere and late.

I'd juist tellt him: "Stop that, and earn yir feed";
but thon curst bruitt, he'd faa doun as he pleased,
sae I gied him a daud on the side of the heid.

Whit happent eftir that, he kinna sneezed,
raxt out his bits of legs, and syne he dee'd.
Wae's me! I'm truly sorry, puir wee beast.

12

RITUAL QUESTIONS

Whan thae twa meet, mind whit I say, Maria.
Staund roun a corner, listen to their spiel.
"Eh-aeh, ma guid auld frien, Maister MacNeill." –
"The same, yir hummil sairvant, Maister McKay."

Says he: "Some sneeshin?" – "Thanks," he says, "I'll try
ae pinch. Hou're ye?" – "Braw, and yirsel?" – "Gey weill,
thank ye." — And syne he says: "Hou dae ye feel,
this weather?" – "Garrs me cheenge ma sarks, och aye."

Says he: "And hou's yir health?" – "Soun as a bell,
and yours?" – "Thank Gode, I'm's weill as maist of men." –
"Yir fowk?" – "Graund; yours?" – "The same, faur's I can tell." –

"I'm glaid of that." – "And I, as ye may ken." –
"Aweill, Maister MacNeill, luik eftir yirsel." –
"Maister McKay . . . till we meet again."

13

A SUGGESTED CEREMONY

Of paipal ploys there arena very monie:
the supper and fuit-weshing hardly staund
fir aa that shuid be duin at Gode's command:
it's time we had a braw new ceremony.

Let's pit in the Paip's neive some kinna wand
or cane, slap on his heid a croun of thorn,
whup him agin a post, treat him wi scorn,
try him and syne condemn him out of haund.

"But there's nae Calvary in Rome," ye say.
If hills ye lack, our city can provide;
we'll hyst the cross up Monte-Mario wey.

And up there, ilka year, at Eastertide,
we'll nail Christ's Vicar on that halie day
forbye twa cardinals, ane on ilk side.

FROM THE FRENCH OF GUILLAUME APOLLINAIRE

VICTORY

A cock craws I'm dreamin and aa the pollards shak
Their leaves that are a semblance of puir seafaring men

Wingit and birlan like Icarus the fause
Sichtless folk waving their airms like ants
Were refleckit by the rain in the plainstanes' mirror

Their lauchs heapt thegither a massy bunch of grapes

Gae nae mair frae my hous my speaking diamond
Sleep doucelie here at hame whaur aathing is your ain
My bed my lamp and my helmet shot throu

See precious sapphires cut some airt about Saint-Claude
    The days were a skire emerant

I am mindfu of ye toun of meteors
They florisht in the air during thae nichts when naething cuid sleep
And the gairdens of the nicht whar I hae gaithert flouers

Ye maun hae eneuch of them to frichtifie yon lyft
    To mind its hiccupin
Ye jalouse wi some difficulty
At whatna pynt success maks a bodie donnert and dozent

They speirit at the institute for the young blin
Hae ye nae blin laddie wi wings

O mouths man is on the luik-out for a new language
To whilk nae grammarian in onie tongue will hae oniething to say

And thae auld leids are that deean-lyk
That it's shairlie throu habit and want of smeddum
That they are still made to sairve for poetrie
But they're like seik folk wi nae smeddum in them
My faith the folk wad suin be dumb aathegither
Miming daes fine in the pictur-hous

    But let's get fou wi speaking
    Shak up the tongue
    Send out postillions

We want new souns new souns new souns
We want consonants wi nae vowels
Consonants that gie smorit farts
    Imitate the soun of a peerie
Firk out a non-stop noise frae your neb
Mak clicks wi your tongue
Mak yuis of the stranglit noise of folk rudely slorpan their meat
The aspirat hechyuch of spittin wad mak anither bonnie consonant
Assortit fisks frae the lips forbye wad mak ye blether like a bugle
Learn to rift at will
And what letter as dowie as a jowan bell
    Awkwart our memories

We cannae hae eneuch delicht
In seein braw new things
O my luve mak haste
Be war of the day when a train steirs your hairt
    Nae mair
Look at it quicker for ye
Thae railways bizzan about
Will suin pass out frae life
They sall be braw and daftlike
Twa lamps brenn fornenst me
Like twa wemen that lauch
Dowie-lyk I bou my heid

Afore the eydent mockage
This lauchter swalls out
Aawhair
Speak wi your hauns snap your fingers
Tap yoursel on the cheek like on a drum
   O words
  They follow amang the myrtle
  Eros and Anteros grietan
I am the lyft owre the city

   D'ye hear the sea

The sea grue faur awa and cry its liefu-lane
  My voice as leal as the shadow
  Ettles aye to be the shadow of life
Ettles to be o sea live traitrous as yoursel

The sea that uncountable sailors has betrayed
Gowpit my huge cries like Hevin's woundit Kings
And the sea to the sunlicht hauds up nocht but shade
That's coost by the sea-maws wi their outspreidan wings
For the word is that sudden a very Gode will shiver
O come and uphaud me I mind wi muckle wae
Those that haud out their airms adoring me thegither
What oasis of airms will gaither me ae day
Dae ye ken of yon joy of seeing aa things new

O voice I'm speaking the language of the sea
In the herbrie by nicht whan the last taverns waik
I mair monie-heidit nor Lerna's water-snake

The street whaur soum my hauns wi ten
Fingers that subtlie probe the toun
Is gane but wha the morn may ken
Whether the street will settle doun
And stop or whit gait I'll gae then
See aa the railways in a dream
Auld-farrant becomin abandonit in a wee while
D'ye see

Victory abuin aa things sall be
To see weill faur awa
To see aathin
Nearhaun
And ilka thing sall hae a new name

FROM THE FRENCH OF HENRI MICHAUX

MY OCCUPATIONS

Ah niver hardly see oniebody bit Aa bash him.

Some folk wad raither hae the interior monologue. No me. Ah like bashin better.

There are folk that sit doun forenenst me in a restaurant and say naething, they bide thair a while, for they've made up their mind to eat.

Here's yin o them.

Aa'll grup ye, hup.

Aa'll better grup ye, hup.

Aa hing him on the hat-rack.

Aa rax him doun.

Aa hing him up again.

Aa rax him doun again.

Aa pit him on the table, Aa stook him and choke him.

Aa fyle him, Aa drouk him.

He's comin tae.

Aa synde him, Aa rax him (Aa'm near wabbit-out, maun gie owre), Aa knead him, Aa wring him, Aa pit him thegither again, and induct him intill ma gless, and ostentatiously teem the glessfu on the flair, and tell the waiter: "Gieze a cleaner gless."

Bit Aa'm feelin no-weill, Aa pey ma bill on the dot, and Aa'm awa.

J. F. Hendry

FROM THE GERMAN OF GOTTFRIED BENN

1

CHOPIN

Not very forthcoming in conversation
Opinions were not his strong point.
Opinions don't get to the root of things.
When Delacroix developed theories
he became ill-at-ease; he was unable himself to provide
a reason for the nocturnes.

As a lover, weak;
shadows in Nohant
where Georges Sand's children
would accept none of his suggestions
about what they should learn.

Tubercular, the type
that is long-drawn out
with haemorrages and scar formation:
a quiet death
as opposed to one
with paroxysmal pain
or at the hands of a firing-squad:
the grand piano (an Erhard) was brought to the door
and Delphine Potocka
sang to him in his last hour
a song about violets.

He travelled to England with three pianos
a Pleyel, an Erhard, a Broadwood
and played for a quarter-of-an-hour in the evening
for 20 guineas
at the Rothschilds' and the Wellingtons', in Stafford House
and before countless Orders of the Garter,
clouded with weariness and approaching death
he would go back home
to the Square d'Orléans.

Then he burnt his sketches
and manuscripts;
no leavings, please, no fragments, notes
or traitorous glimpses
at the end he said:
"My efforts have been brought to a conclusion
insofar as it lay in my power."

Every finger was to play
with the strength built into its structure:
the fourth is the weakest
(just a Siamese twin to the middle finger).
When he began they lay on E, F sharp, G sharp, B natural and C.

No one who ever heard some
of his Preludes
whether in country-houses or
in the hills
or through French windows on to terraces,
a sanatorium's for instance,
will find it easy to forget.

Never an opera composed,
and not one symphony:
only these tragic progressions
out of artistic conviction
and with a hand that was small.

2

ASTERS

Asters – days that smoulder
old enchantment, spells,
for one hesitant hour
the gods hold the scales.

Once again the golden horde
heaven, light and blossoming,
and what is old genesis brooding
on, beneath her dying wings?

Once again, what you longed for
ecstasy, the "you" in the rose –
summer, stock-still, leaning over
to look out at the swallows.

Once again, apprehension of all,
replacing certainty long alert,
the floods the swallows skirt
drinking their journey in, and nightfall.

3

WORDS

Alone: you: with words
and that is really alone.
There trumpets and triumphal
arches are unknown.

You look into their soul
for the original, primal features
year after year: stop torturing
yourself: you won't find anything.

And lights are shining across the way
in some moist, tender arbour
and moist and rosy lips unconsciously
let fall the pearl of the word.

It is only your years turn yellow
in another sense
away into dreams: syllabic —
while you steal, silent, away.

4

NEVER LONELIER THAN IN AUGUST

Never lonelier than in August –
time of fulfilment – the countryside
ablaze with fires of gold and red
but where is pleasure in your gardens?

The lakes are bright, the heavens mild
the fields are fresh and glisten softly
but where are the triumphs and the trophies
from the realm you represent?

Where proof of everything is – happiness
and glances are exchanged and rings
a wine's bouquet, the rapture of things
you serve the spirit – its antithesis.

Douglas Young

FROM THE GREEK OF SAPPHO

TIL ANAKTORIA

Maik o the gods he seems to me,
thon man that sits in front o ye,
and hears your talkan couthilie near,
sae saftlie and clear,

your luvelie lauchan. My hert stounds
rowsan i ma breist when your lauch sounds,
and gif I glent at ye sittan there
I canna speak mair.

Ma tung freezes i ma mou, a nesh
lowe rins chitteran throu ma flesh;
nae sicht i ma een; wi their nain thunner
ma lugs dunner.

Swyte reems doun me; frae heid to fuit
a trummlan grups me, sae's I sit
greener nor gerss, in sic a dwalm
I kenna wha I am.

FROM THE ITALIAN OF DANTE ALIGHIERI

Ae time that I our flownrie life appraisit
and saw how brief and bruckil its duratioun,
i ma hert, whaurin he wones, Luve sabbit sairlie,
and wi Luve's sabban then my saul was frazit,
sae that I sychit and spak in conturbatioun:
"Siccar my luve maun dee, maun dee fu shairly".
At thocht o that I was dumbfoundert fairlie,
I steekit my een, that were forfairn and drowie,
and my hale spreit was dowie,
ilk facultie disjeskit and forwandert.
Syne as I ponderit,
frae trowth and kennan furth forvayt unwarelie,
phantouns o brayn-wud weemen drave at me,
and skraugh, "Yoursel maun dee. Ay, ye maun dee".

Then saw I monie a dubie ferly, glaikit
wi slidder phantasies I gaed amang.
I kenna in whatna rowm I seemit to be,
whaur sheylit weemen cam stravaigan, traikit
wi makan waefu mane and greetan lang,
whas een wi grame flaughterit maist fierilie.
Howdlins a mirk owrehailt the sun's bricht blee,
the starns atour the firmament sae lither
waementit ilk til ither;
I saw the birds fleean i the lyft doun drap,
the hale yird quok and lap.
Syne cam a deid-wan chiel, spak hairsilie:
"Hae ye na heard the bruit o it frae onie?
Deid is your leddie, that was verra bonny".

FROM THE FRENCH OF PAUL VALÉRY

THE KIRKYAIRD BY THE SEA

This lown riggin-side, whaur whyte doos gang,
quhidders amang the pines, the graves amang;
thonder perjink midday compounds frae fires
the sea, the sea, that 's aye begun anew.
Braw guerdon eftir musardry to view
canny and lang the verra Gods' lown lires.

Wi what pure wark fine fuddrie-leams consume
monie an unseen diamant frae the spume.
Hou lown a peace is kendlit keethanlie.
When the sun liggs abune the abysm o swaws,
pure craturs o an everbydan cause,
time skinkles and the dream is savendie.

Savendle thesaur, Pallas' simple shrine,
thou mass o calm, seen siccar no to crine,
proud gloweran watter, ee that hains inside
sae meikle sleep ablow a fiery pall,
O my ain lownness! . . . Biggin i the saul,
thousand-tiled gowden summit. Riggin-side!

41

Time's temple that a single sych can sum,
to this pure point I sclim, I'm uisd to come,
encircled wi my sea-stravaigan glance;
and like my final offerin to the Gods
thon seelfu skinklin saws, like grain on clods,
owre the deep hicht a sovran arrogance.

As a fruct dwynes awa at a bite,
turnan its absence til a delyte
intil a mou whaur its form smoors,
I am braithan here my future fume,
and the luift sings to the saul gane tuim
the turnin to tumult o thir shores.

Braw luift, true luift, luik at me as I change.
Eftir sae meikle pride, sae meikle strange
thowlessness, and yet fou o virr,
I gie mysel owre to this gesserant spase.
On the deid fowk's houses my shadaw gaes,
makan me chief wi its dwaiblie steer.

My saul laid bare to the solstice-brands,
I haud ye up, wi your pitiless hands
thou wonderfu justice o siccan licht.
I restore you pure to your first place.
Luik at me! . . . But reflectin rays
requires a dull half o shadaw-nicht.

For me my lane, me lane, in mysel
by a hert, whaur the springs o poetry well,
atween tuimness and the pure event,
I byde on the echo o my inner pouer,
wersh cistern, sonorous, obscure,
soundan i the saul a chasm never rent.

Do ye ken, fause prisoner o fullyeries,
gulph that swalws thir thin trellises,
owre my steekit een, secrets that blin,
what corse trails me til its thowless end,
what brou draws it to this bane-rife grund?
A bit sperk thonder thinks o my absent kin.

Steekit, consecrat, fou o fire but fuel,
a fragment o yird offered to the licht's rule,
I like this place, wi its brands' royal waves,
biggit frae gowd and stane and derk-leaved glades,
whaur fouth o marble sooms owre fouth o shades,
thonder the leal sea sleeps atour my graves.

C'wa my grand bitch! gar misbelievers skail!
When I'm my lane smilean I tell my tale
o ferlie sheep lang I hae herdit here,
the whyte flock o thir my laigh lown lairs.
Keep aff the doos wi their auld-farrant airs,
and thowless dreams, and angels gleg to speir.

Aince here, the future is but indolence.
The golloch-scartit drouth liggs here intense.
Aathing brunt up, forduin, taen intil air,
intil ane essence stark ayont our thocht. . . .
Life becomes merchless, fou wi want o ocht,
wershness is douce, the spreit is clear and rare.

The dernit deid ligg cozy in this yird,
that warms and dries their mystery interred.
Midday abune, Midday without a steer
thinks in himsel, self-congruent, cordial. . . .
Thou complete heid and perfect coronal,
I am the secret change inside you here.

You've nane but me to haud in check your fears.
My penitence, compulsion, douts and fears
the flaw to tash your diamant's majestie.
But in their nicht, wechtit wi marble stane,
a drowie fowk doun at the tree-ruits lain
hae sideit wi you in slaw solemnitie.

They hae dwyneit intil a thick nonentitie,
the reid clay drank the whyte identitie,
the gift o life has gane intil the fleurs.
Whaur are the deid anes' turns o phrase we kent,
their individual sauls, their personal sclent?
The larva spins in the tears' auld course.

Kittlit lassies' skreighins, blyth and keen,
bricht whyte teeth, blue and greetan een,
the loesome breist whaur the reid lowelicht lay,
the bluid that leams frae the surrendered mou,
the final gifts, the hands that guaird them true,
aa gangs to grund and comes again in play.

And you, great saul, do you hope for some dream
that sanna hae this bricht delusive leam
made here for carnal een by the gowd and the sea?
D'ye think ye'll sing when ye're a reekie wraith?
Fegs! Aathing flees! Here's me a porous graith!
And mystical Impatience tae maun dee!

Sable and gilt, thin Immortality,
thou lykewauk-kimmer, laureat monstrouslie,
makan o cauldruif daith a mither's lap,
the bonny lee, the pious stratagem!
Wha kensna them, wha scunnersna at them?
This tuim beld skull, this ever-girnan chap!

Profound faithers, ye untenantit skulls,
dounwechtit we sae monie shuilfulls,
wha are the yird and taigle up our feet,
the true smurler, the worm nane can dodd,
is no for you, sleepan ablow the brod,
he lives on life, my life, and winna lea 't!

Luve, aiblins, or self-hate, it may be?
His secret tooth is come sae near to me
that onie name could set him weel the day.
Why fash? He sees, desires, taks thocht, and grips!
He likes my flesh, he sups wi nuptial lips.
skairin his life is aa the life I hae!

Zeno, cruel maister of Eleatic thocht,
hae ye thirlit me wi thon arrow aflocht,
that dirls and flees and doesna flee a bit?
The sound bairns me and the arrow slays.
And the sun, Och! . . . a tortoise-shadaw's pace
for the saul, Achilles stickit wi fiery fuit!

Na, na! Stand up! Intil the time aheid!
Brak up, my bouk, this pose o thochtfu heed!
Drink, apen breist, the newborn wind's upspring.
A sudden freshness, a breith frae aff the sea,
gies me my saul again. . . . Saut potencie!
C'wa, let us rin to the swaw wi virrfu fling.

Ay, meikle sea, deliriouslie arrayed,
thou panther-hide, thou gairit goddess-plaid
o myriad myriad solar deities,
absolute Hydra, fou wi your blue lire,
bitean your tail o skinklan sperks o fire
amang a dirdum lown as silence is.

44

The wind wins up! . . . I maun ettle to live!
The merchless air apens and steeks my breve.
Abune the craigs swaw-pouther daurs be sprayed.
Flee awa nou, ye licht-bumbazeit blads.
Brak, brak, ye swaws. Brak wi blyth water-flads
this lown riggin-side whaur reivan jibsails gaed!

G. S. Fraser

FROM THE LATIN OF HORACE

ODE

Look at the shine of snow up there upon
Soracte, where the labouring boughs
    Sag with their load, and bleak
    Winter has blocked the streams.

Here, melt this rigour, scattering logs
High on the hearth; then trundle out,
    Grandly, the Sabine jars
    Of strong wine, four years old.

Leave to the gods the rest; who, when
They have allayed upon the boiling deep
    These skirmishers, frail ash
    And cypress cease to shake.

Stop searching into sad to-morrow and
What day Luck now may grant, count that
    As cash, Child, do not scorn
    Gay dalliance or the dance.

So long as sour old age his distance keeps.
Now in the Campus Martius and the squares
    Is the time for twilight
    Whispers of assignation

For the laugh from a far off corner
Of a lurking girl who defends her
    Forearm and her fingers
    In a mock-modest way.

FROM THE LATIN OF TIBULLUS

ELEGY

How well I'd bear the break, my anger spoke it:
Nothing more distant than defiance now!
Now, with a quick and clever boy to whip me,
I'm whirling like a top across the flags!

Brand my wild heart, and hurt it, that hereafter
It love not bragging: tame my bristling words!
And yet be kind. How once we put together
Our heads, made furtive plots, were fond, recall!
Think, when you lay cast down by wretched sickness,
Who was it sprinkled cleansing sulphur round,
And who invoked, lest mournful dreams beset you,
Quiet sleep, thrice scattering the sacred meal?
Cowled, in loose tunic, through the small hours' silence,
Who at the crossroads made the ninefold vow?
This payment mine, another has the profit,
Lucky, who draws the interest on my prayers!
I feigned, poor frantic man (the gods unfriendly!)
I should be happy then, if you were safe.

"Life on the land! Let Delia watch my harvests,
While on the hot, hard floor they thresh the corn,
Or watch the clusters in the full vat heaping
When rapid feet tread out the shiny must;
And learn to count my flocks; and, as a loving
Mistress, to dandle talkative small slaves;
Learn to give grapes as offering for vintage,
Spiked ears in pledge for corn, brimmed bowls for flocks.
She'll manage every man and every matter
And leave no task for me in all my house.
Messalla visits us . . . the sweetest apples
Delia will pluck him from the choicest trees:
Such a great man, she'll be an anxious hostess,
Prepare and serve his meals, a waiting maid!"

Such were my dreams that now the crosswinds carry
To scatter in Armenia's scented vales!

Often with drink I seek to rout these sorrows,
But sorrow turns wine itself to tears,
Often with girls; but on joy's very margin
Love, that recalls my love, abandons me.
The one who leaves me then will talk of witchcraft,
And say — oh, shame! – you know unholy charms!
And yet it is not words that could bewitch me,
But looks, soft arms, and girlish golden hair:
Such to Haemonian Peleus once was Thetis,
The sea-blue Nereid on her bridled fish!
These charms could charm me!

Some rich lover wants you,
And his accomplice is some crafty bawd!
May blood defile her food, her mouth be bloody
As it gluts brewage mingled with much gall!
May ghosts around her ply, their plight bemoaning,
Yes, and the ghoul-bird skirl upon her roof!
Let her pluck grass from graveyards, dogged by hunger,
Seek pickings from the morsels left by wolves,
Howl through the streets with nothing round her middle,
Run at the crossways from wild yelping dogs!
So be it! A god confirms. Powers guard lovers.
Venus, renounced for no just cause, will rage.
So, Delia, leave this witch's griping lessons
In time, in time . . .

In love must riches win?
For your poor man is your most trusty servant,
Your poor man soonest cleaves to your soft side,
Your poor man, in the crush, a sturdy comrade,
Pushes your hips and somehow makes a way,
Your poor man will draw off your muddy leggings
And loose the coverings from your snowy feet.

(I sing in vain! Fine words will not win open
That door, who knocks must have a plenteous hand!)

You, who carry the day, of my fate be wary!
Light Luck turns lightly on her turning wheel.
Not in vain now one waits at the threshold,
Patient, and looks about him, and withdraws,
And seems to pass the house, but soon returning
Will hawk himself at Delia's very doors!
Sly Love has a dodge afoot. Be gay, I beg you,
While you can: your sloop still bobs in a clear sea!

FROM THE LATIN OF CATULLUS

1

Dear Lesbia, let us live and love,
Never thinking twopence of
All these grumbling grim old men,
Suns go down, come up again:
Down but once goes our brief light
Into one perpetual night.
A thousand kisses, then a hundred,
Then a thousand and a hundred,
A hundred on a thousand pour!
When we've many thousand more
Let us muddle up the score.
Bad men might count every kiss
And might envy us our bliss.

2

Varus, you know Suffenus well. He is
Handsome, and quite a wit, and nicely mannered,
And the most copious scribbler in the world.
He must have written quite ten thousand verses,
Or more, and not like other folk on scraps,
But on imperial paper, in new rolls,
New bosses, fine red ribbon, parchment covers,
All ruled with lead, and all smoothed out with pumice.
And when you read these, this smooth pretty fellow
Suddenly seems a goatherd or a navvy:
It's so absurd and such a total change.
What shall we say about this? Here's a man
More than just bright and gay and affable
Who suddenly becomes a hick of hicks
Taking to poetry: yet a man who's never
Really so happy as when writing poems:
That's what he likes and worships in himself.
Well, we all fall this way. There's not a person
Whom in some matter you can fail to see
To be Suffenus. Each has his own pet maggot:
We cannot see what hangs behind our backs.

3

If there's some pleasure in remembering
the decent things one did (that one felt true,
and broke no serious oath, and in no compact
used the god's greatness for deceiving men),
then, in a long life, many joys, Catullus,
are surely due you for your squandered love!
All gentle things a man can say or do
in love, by you have all been said or done:
all, to a thankless heart entrusted, perished.

Why do you still extend your area of
self-torture? Why not stiffen up, draw back,
and cease – the gods dislike it – to be wretched?
It's hard to quench an old love suddenly:
it's hard, indeed, but what you've got to do:
you must do this, whether you can or not!
Gods, if there's pity in you, or if ever
to any deathbed you brought any comfort,
have pity on poor me! Was my life honest?
Then snatch away this plague and ruin from me –
alas, this slackness in my deepest joints,
creeping that drives my heart's delight away!
I ask no longer this: for my love, her love:
nor wish she'd wish, though vainly, to be chaste.
I want mere health: to lay down this vile sickness.
If I've observed decorum, gods, grant this!

FROM THE ITALIAN OF GUIDO CAVALCANTI

SONNETS

1

My foolish eyes, that first did look upon,
Lady, your all too formidable face,
Were those that did accuse me of you, on
A day when Love held court in his high place;
And laid their evidence before him there
That by his judgement I should be your slave –
What sighs and griefs did down upon me bear
And what a rashness in my heart did rave!
Then led me forth again, all pleas denied,

Into a place where seemed it there was none
But for Love's burden drew a sighing breath:
Who, when they saw me, all with pity cried,
"Now you are made the slave of such a one
That other hope you cannot have than Death!"

2

Who's this that comes, as each man looks at her,
Makes tremulous with clarity the air,
And leads Love with her, so that speak or stir
Can none among us: all have sighs to spare!
Alas? How seems she when her eyes she turns?
Let Love relate what I may not explain:
Yet such esteem her modest bearing earns
Another in her place shall earn disdain.
Uncounted are the gifts that make her rich:
To her the Gentle Virtues are obeisant:
Beauty, as Beauty's Goddess, doth approve her.
Nor was our mind tuned to so high a pitch,
Nor of its health so properly complaisant,
That we could have a proper knowledge of her.

3

Beauty of ladies of compassionate heart
And cavaliers, in arms, and high in pride,
And singing birds, and lovers' rhetoric art,
And painted ships which on the strong seas ride,
And air serene at the first peep of dawn,
And blanched snow descending with no wind,
And watery bank, and flower-adorned lawn,
And ornaments with azure and gold refined,
So much her beauty and her nobleness
Surpass, and such a courage do they carry,
Those seem but stale in the beholder's eye:
So much more knowledge in her looks doth lie
As the low earth than the high heaven is less:
To such a one good luck will never tarry.

51

FROM THE FRENCH OF STEPHANE MALLARMÉ

The virgin, bright, and beautiful to-day
Dare it now shatter with a drunken wing
This hard, forgotten lake, this ice where cling
These flights of mine that never flew away . . .
Once was a swan, remembers it is he,
Magnificent but hopeless in his strife,
For never having sung the realms of life
When winter shone in bleak sterility.
His neck in a white agony is shaken,
Shattering the space that mocks him for his pride,
But not the soil in which his plumes are taken.
Phantom mere brightness to this scene has drawn,
Immobile in the cold, where dreams deride,
Clothed in the useless exile of the swan.

George Campbell Hay

FROM THE ITALIAN OF CECCO ANGIOLIERI

SONNETS

1

Gin I war eld, this warld wi flames I'd ring it,
gin wund, I'd scraich an' rant an' birle't aroond,
gin watter, droon it whar nae man could soond,
gin I war God, doon thro the luft I'd ding it.

Gin I war Pope o Rome I wad be merry,
makin gowks o ma flock sae lown an' wae.
Gin I war Emprour, ken ye what I'd dae?
Shave ilkane's heid as bare's a rowan berry.

Gin I war Daith I'd seek ma faither's dure;
gin Life, I'd rin lik stoor an' jink the knave.
Sae wi ma mither. Baith are stieve an' soor.

Gin I war Cecco – I'm that, may God me save –
I'd lift ilk bonny lass (had I the poo'r)
an' lea the auld an' ugsome tae the lave.

2

What luck is waur than mine, that kenna why
I canna gie owre looan, downa lea
ane wha, cauld hater, disna care for me
eneuch tae turn her heid whan I gang bye.

She chills me wi her glances norlan-snell,
she maks me sweit wi anguish nicht an' day,
an' sets ma sawl ableeze, garran me say:
"Ither than this, there *is* nae ither Hell."

Ye thriep, "Ye'll win nae guid frae ocht she daes.
Sic come they aa frae Eve." Wi truth ye say't.
I ken the bruckle waveran o their ways.

Yet, daft wi looan, wycer ne'er a hait,
I luik tae Luve tae flooer her frozen braes.
Strang Luve, e'en in the bygaun He can dae't.

53

3

Far mair than aa the watters o the sea,
saut wave on wave, repentance droons ma cheer,
syne – blate tho lief – I daurna tak the floo'r
that in a kindly blink she offert me.

On her alane her Maker set his ee,
forgettan aathing else, an' med her fair –
an' gin ye say: "Doitit, luve-blint ye are,"
then gang an' hear her speak, gang, luik an' see.

An' I wull ken ye hae a hert o stane
gin ye come back but Luve frae luikan there,
an' say: "Yere sonnet lees, Cecco ma man."

She has a face sae fine, sae kind an air,
that in the warld her peer is her alane.
Why was it born, thon face ablow thon hair?

4

Aye, I hae focht wi Luve an' Luve liggs deid;
an' vext I am he lastit oot sae lang.
Yet I was in the richt, he in the wrang,
an' sae 'twas siccar Fate wad snap his threid.

"I'se blaw ye tae the port whar ye wad be,"
he said, then sent a fause, unchancy breeze,
ettlan (gin I had lippent tae his lees)
tae foonder me, wandert far oot at sea.

Aften, afore oor warslean-hauds war brokkin,
I fand him strang an' glegg eneuch tae gie
mony a dizzy cloor an' reuchlik rockan.

Aften, in truth, he aamaist feenisht me,
yet at the end o't, wasna worth a docken,
for Cecco killt him cauld, an' sae gaed free.

FROM THE ITALIAN OF FRANCESCO PETRARCA

SONNET

Luve wiled me back, promisan nocht but weel,
an' brocht me til thon prison kent o auld,
an' gied the keys o it tae hae an' hauld
tae her, wha drives me yet oot frae masel.
Wae's me! I didna see his drift until
baith had me boond. Noo, fechtan aye an' feart –
but wha will lippen tae me, thoch I sweir't –
I hae wan back tae freedom, seichan still.
I, lik a prisoner, yet bear a dale
o ma auld chains upon me an' ma scathe,
an' ma hert's pain-shaws clear on broo an een.
Wha sees me swaiver bye sae gash an' pale
will say: "Gin I can read what I hae seen,
thonder gaed ane had stude richt close tae daith".

FROM THE CROATIAN OF FRANO ALFIREVIĆ

SOLDIERS' GRAVEYARD

All life is one. Soft whispering the tall grass lifts and bows.
The sky they sleep beneath is radiant as God's face.
I search for the last brief thought of their nameless, shattered brows,
as I pass by the rotting crosses in this forgotten place.

What ages have sown the earth with the bones of our wandered kind,
for Country, or God or King, in battles lost and won,
and for things half understood that live on to prick the mind,
some urge that stirs as we watch the wounded evening sun.

They would loom up and stand like mountains across the sky,
the scattered bones of the ages, were they gathered into one.
With a glance of human feeling I unite them where they lie,
those enemies at peace in the earth, their hating done.

The peasants come from the fields. With laughter and talk they pass;
their strangely living voices die in this quiet of death.
Did it truly happen here? I walk the dewy grass,
my bitter thoughts below with the dead, and I check my breath.

Here lies the cherished life that mothers gifted, crushed.
Here a man is less than nothing among such myriad dead.
Yet each of them was a world, and who knows but this scattered dust
lived hot days of grandeur in their wars unwritten, unread.

I grieve from the dim defeats in battles of days long gone.
Here dreams, that might have been born in deeds, lie overthrown.
In vain their life and death? Ah no, their land lived on,
and their hearts still beat in songs, while here they sleep unknown.

The trains roar past the field screaming with lights ablaze;
bearing east and west scheming and wealth they fly.
Who mocks the fallen dead while grave silence speaks their praise?
Yet life in haste unheeding with the gods and beasts goes by.

Sydney Goodsir Smith

FROM THE FRENCH OF TRISTAN CORBIÈRE

THE GANGREL RYMOUR AND THE PAIRDON OF SANCT ANNE

Sainit is the fouthless shore
Whar, like the sea, aa is nude,
Hailie is the fremmit kirk
O' Sanct Anne-de-la-Palud,

O' the Guidwife Sanct Anne,
Guid-Auntie til the bairnie Jesus,
In the rotten wuid o her soutane
Rich, mair rich nor Croesus.

By her, the shelpit wee Virgin,
A spindle, onwytes the *Angelus*;
Joseph, wi his candle, skouks in a neuk,
Nane nou to fête his sanctliness.

*

It is the Pairdon – blythness and mysteries –
The cowit gerss is routh wi lice. . . .
– *Sanct Anne, consolatioun o spouses,*
Balm o the guid wifes!

Frae Plougastel and Loc-Tudy,
The burghs round about,
Fowk comes to set their tents,
Three days and nichts — or Monday's out.

Three days, three nichts the muir graens
Heedan the auld ritual,
– Seraphic choir and drucken sang –
The SPIRITUAL CANTICLE.

*

O, Mither hackit frae hairt o aik,
Dour and guid, wi dunts o an axe,
Aneath the gowd o her robe she derns
Luve in the likeness o Breton francs!

– Auld Greenie wi the face worn
Like a stane wi the fluid,
Runkelt wi the tears o luve,
Crynit wi the greit o bluid!

– Thou whas skruckenit breist
Remade for itsel –
Haean cairrit Mary's virginitie –
The virginitie o a male!

– Proud servant-maistress
Hie amang the maist hie;
But, til the puir world, unproud,
Leddie fou o proprietie!

A kent for the blind! A crutch
For the auld! For the newborn an airm!
Mither o the Leddie your dochter!
Mither o ilka vagabairn!

– O, Flouer o the young virgin!
Fruct o the wife wi muckle breist!
Leddie o Mercies for the wedow-man!
For the wedow-woman an altar o peace!

– Ark o Joachim! Ancestral mither!
A medal o forworn bress, ye!
Hailie mistle! Fowr-leafit clover!
Mount o Horeb! Seed o Jesse!

–O, thou that smoorit the grieshoch,
That spun as we did at hame,
When the gloamin begood to faa,
Haudan on your knaps the Wean;

Thou workan there your lane, to mak
His bairnie-clouts at Bethlehem,
And there to stitch his mort-claith
Sae doulie at Jerusalem!

Your runkles are deep corses,
White as cotton your hair . . .
Haud aff the Ill Ee o yeldness
Frae the crib o wir bairns' bairns. . . .

Gar thae come, and hain them blythfullie,
That are unborn and that are here,
And, when God isna lookan,
Owre the damned pour out your tears!

Tak back in their white gounies
The bairns that are seick and hangie,
Cry back til an ayebydan Sabbath
The auld that trauchle wearilie.

—Dragon-chaperone o the Virgin,
Guaird the crib wi your ee,
While by ye Joseph the porter
Guairds the house's respectabilitie!

Hae ruth for the mither-lassie
And the bairn at the roadside . . .
Gin onie cast a stane
Gar it cheynge intil breid!

– Leddie that's guid by sea and land,
Shaw us the luift and the harberie,
In war and in tourbillioun
Lantren o the guid daith are ye!

Lawlie: ye've no a sterne at your fuit,
Lawlie . . . and wurdie for hainin aa!
Your veil furthshaws in the luift,
Peril's blae aureola.

– Til the faaen whas life is gray
(Faaen – pairdon me – wi the drink taen)
Furthshaw the knock on the kirk touer
And the road hame.

Lend thy douce and saikless gleid
Til thir Christian sauls. . . .
And your auld wife's remeids
As weill til thy hornit bestial!

Shaw our wemen and servant-lassies
Dargs and fecunditie. . . .
– A handsel til our auld folks' sauls
E'en nou in Eternitie!

– We'se set ye a ring o candles,
O' brent-new yalla candles, round
Your kirk, and we sall tell
Your Laich Mass at skreak-o-dawin.

Hap thou wir riggintree
Frae the Deil's work and ilka freit . . .
At Pace ye'se be gien
A mirligae and some threid.

Gin our bodies stink upo the yerth
A halesome bath is the grace o ye:
Pour out upon us in the mools
Thy guid odour o sanctitie.

– Till a towmond! – Here's your candle:
Twa pund it set me!
Respecks til my Leddie the Virgin,
No forgettan the Trinitie.

*

And, shauchlan on their knaps,
The faithfu in their sarks –
Sanct Anne, hae pitie on us! –
Gang thrice round the kirk,

And drink the hailie water
Whar the sca'd-heid Jobs hae lauvit
Their smittle naukitness. . . .
Gang your weys! Faith has ye sauvit!

It's there the puir foregaither,
The brether o Jesus.
– It's no the court o miracles,
The holes are real: Vide latus!

Are they no divine on their hurdles?
Haloes round aureoles o vermeelion,
Thir proprietors o scurls,
In the sun the live cornelians! . . .

Houlan, a rachitic
Shaks a baneless stump,
Joustlan an epileptic
That works in a sump.

There, beilins grow on the runt o a man,
Here, mistle on the runt o a tree,
Here, a lassie and her mither
Dansan Sanct Vitus's jiggerie.

Anither shaws the shanker
O' her infeckit wean:
He auchts it his faither. . . .
Nou the breidwinner's the blane.

Yonder's a born naitural,
Ane o Sanct Gabriel's visitatioun,
In the ecstasie o saiklessness . . .
– And gey near salvatioun! –

– But, bycomer, look! Aathing bygaes.
Lown is the naitural's ee,
For he's in the state o grace . . .
– And Grace is Eternitie! –

Efter vespers, amang the lave
Sprent wi hailie water, a cadaver
Thrives, livan by leprosie,
– Memento o some crusader . . .

And aa thae that the Kings o France
Made haill wi a finger's pressure . . .
– But France has nae mair kings,
And their God hauds back his pleisure.

– Cheritie in their bedesman-bouls!
Thegither our forebears hae cairrit
Thae fleurs-de-lys o scrofulie
That the elect inherit.

Miserere for the revels
O' the cancers and the lippers!
Thae crutches can dunt ye,
Thae runts there are nippers.

Hae a shot, then, ye gleg yins,
But tak tent o your skin:
Mynd thae boulie shanks – and airms! –
In the Kyrie eleison!

. . . And, lassie, that's come to watch
And tak the air, turn awa!
Aiblins frae out the ither rags
The rags o flesh will shaw. . . .

For they hunt there, on their estates!
Their pelts are their gowpan scutcheons:
– The richt o the Laird til their claws! . . .
– The richt o the Lord in-ben!

Stacks o *ex votos* o rotten meat,
Carnel-house o the elect for salvatioun,
In the Lord's house they are at hame!
– Are they no his creatioun?

They thrang in the yerdin-grund,
Ye'd think the deid had gane agait
Haean ruggit frae neath the stanes
Nocht but limbs ill-set.

– *We* – we maun wheesht! *They* are sauntit:
It is the wyte o Adam's sin,
By the finger o the Abune they're brandit:
Blessit be the hand o the Abune!

Scapegaets o the muckle riff-raff
Here ablow loddenit wi forfauts,
On them God outbocks his wrath! . . .
– The minister o Sanct Anne is fat.

*

But ae braithless note,
An echo trummlan on the wind,
Comes to brash the drizzenan drune
O' this stravaigan limbo-grund.

A human bouk, that's rairan,
Stands by the Calvarie;
It looks like ane hauf-blind;
Wi nae tyke and but ae ee. . . .

It's a gangrel rymour
That gies the fowk, for a farden,
The Ballant o the Vagabone Yid,
Abelard, or *The Magdalen.*

Breathan like a dredgie,
Like a dredgie o hunger itsel,
And, dreich as a day wantan breid,
Dowilie, its wail. . . .

Wae bird, wantan fedder or nest,
It sings as it breathes,
Round the puirs'-houses o granite
Vaigan whar instinct leads. . . .

Doutless it can speak tae,
And, juist as it sees, can think:
Afore it aye the hie road . . .
And, when there's tuppence, there's drink;

A woman, it looks; wae's me! – her clouts
Hing frae her, wi twine upkiltit:
Her black tooth hauds a pipe, gane out . . .
– Life's aye some consolation intil't!

Her name? – She's cried Miserie.
Hap saw her birth, and yerth
Will see her daith . . . nae
Differ – for the maist pairt.

Gin ye should meet wi her, makar,
Wi her auld sodjer's poke:
It's our sister . . . gie her – it's holidays –
A bit baccy, for a smoke!

Ye'll see her runklie face runkle
Wi a smile, as in a tree;
And her sca'd hand will make
A true sign o the Cross for ye.

THE TWAL

I

Mirk the nicht,
White the snaw,
The snell wind blaws,
Ca'an aa fowk doun –
The snell wind blaws
Throu aa God's mapamound.

Frae the white grund
The yowden-drift
Blaws in lacy wreithes,
Under the snaw is ice –
Slidder and glaizie. . . .
Aabodie skites around
And doun they faa
Puir craturs aa!

Frae house til house, athort the causie,
A raip is straucht whar sweys
A muckle hingan clout that tells ye:
ALL POUER TIL THE CONSTITUENT ASSEMBLIE!

An auld wife's sair fashed wi this;
She's greitan; she canna get what it means.
    What for's the muckle banner, then?
    Siccan a michtie swatch o claith?
    It'd dae for leggins for the weans,
    Maist aa o them's wantan claes. . . .

        Like a hen the auld wife
        Teeters across the snaw. . . .
        O, Mither o God, thae Bolshies
        'll be the daith o us aa!

        The wind like a whip!
        The frost like a knife –
        A bourgeois at the corner
        Haps his neb in his coat-collar.

64

But wha's this? Wi the buss o hair,
Girnan under his braith:
    Traitors! he says,
    Russia's betrayit!
– He'll be a scryvor,
A pennie-a-liner . . .

And yonder's a lang-gounied fellie
Stravaigan yonder by the snaw-wreithe. . . .
Are ye no brawlie thae days,
    Brither meenister?
Are ye myndan the guid auld times
When ye strode wi stuck-out bellie
And the Cross upo' your weym
    Glentit on aa men? . . .

Yonder's a leddie wi an Astrakhan coat
Bletheran wi a woman friend –
Ay, my dear, and we grat and grat . . .
    And she slips!
    Crash! – Airse owre tip!
– Oh, michtie me! – I' the name . . . !
Heave awa, lads! Up wi her! Up!

The snell wind's feelan grand,
Ramskeerie and blye –
It blaws up lassies' skirts
And blaws doun passers-by,
The muckle banner it ryves in twae,
Shogs and shaks it and blaws it agley.
ALL POUER TIL THE CONSTITUENT ASSEMBLIE!

– And, on the wind ye hear:
. . . We had an assemblie, tae . . .
. . . In yonder muckle haa . . .
. . . Had a grand discussion . . .
. . . Passed a resolution . . .
. . . Ten bob for a short-time, a quid for the nicht . . .
. . . And no a tanner less . . .
. . . C'mon, let's doss . . .

The nicht's weiran on,
The causie tuim,
Anerlie a vagabone
Shauchles around.
– *And the souch o the wind . . . !*

Hey, ye tink!
Come here –
I'll no *eat* ye . . . !
Here's a bit breid!
– And what neist
For the likes o me?
– Och, tae hell wi ye!

The lift is mirk, mirk.

Hate, dowie hate
Teems in the breist . . .
Mirkie hate, hailie hate. . . .

Brither!
   Tak tent!

II

The storm roves on: the snaw swirls round . . .
Twal men are mairchan throu the toun.
Their rifle-slings are black . . .
Around them fires, lichts, in the mirk.

Fags in their mous and bannets a-cock,
They should hae Braid Arrows on their backs.
         Freedom! Freedom! Libertie!
         Nae Kirk for me!
         Aroo! Aroo! Aree!
      It's gey cauld, fellies, gey cauld!

Johnnie's gane til the howff wi Kate . . .
In her stockin she's siller eneuch for them baith.

And Johnnie's got lashings . . . I'm tellan *you*!
He was aince ane o us – he's a sodjer nou!

Weill, Johnny, ye bystart plutocrate,
Juist you try and taigle wi my wee Kate!

      Freedom! Freedom! Libertie!
      Nae Kirk for me!

Kittie's gey chief wi Johnnie the nou!
And what wad her business be – the cou!

      Taradiddle! Aroo! Aroo!

Aa around us gleids are glinkan . . .
Across our shouthers rifles hingan . . .

Watch your step, my traistie fiere!
The enemie sleeps gey lichtlie here!

Brither, tak your gun i' your hand!
A round for Hailie Russia, man!
    Russia the raucle-hairtit —
    Russia o the wuiden cots –
    Russia wi the muckle hurdies!

    – Nae Kirk for me!

III

Ay, and sae wir laddies are went
A-servan wi the Reid Guaird –
A-servan wi the Reid Guaird –
Their rampish heids'll sune be tint!

We's wearie-wae, nae dout,
But life is fun!
Wi a raggit greatcoat
And an Austrian gun!

Ay, we sall fire a michtie gleid
And wae for the bourgeoisie around us!
Throu aa the world a gleid o bluid –
Wi the blessing o' the Lord upon us!

IV

The snaw swirls, a cabbie yalls,
Johnnie wi Kittie hurlan by,
Bleezan lamps to licht their wey . . .
    On ye gae, then, on ye gae! . . .

In his sodjer's greatcoat Johnnie's braw
Wi a daftlike grin upo his maw,
Twirlan and twirlan his mustachiaw!
    Twirlan it up and doun
    Daffan like a loun . . .

Eh, what a braw lad is our John!
Ech, what a gift o' the gab has John!
See nou, she's in his airms – the hure!
He's talkan her round . . . and round . . .
and owre . . .

Kittie flings her heid back nou,
Teeth white as pearls in a bluid-reid mou . . .
Ach, my Kittie! Ach, my hinnie!
Wi your round wee mug sae bonnie!

v

On your craig, my Kittie,
My dirk-scaur winna heal –
Ablow your bub, my Kittie,
Anither skaith as weill!

Hey, jig a jig, O jig for me!
Silken shanks are guid to see!

Ye flichterit round in slips o lace –
Flichter round, then, aa ye wish!
Wi officers set a bonnie pace –
Gang the pace, then, aa ye wish!

Hey jig a jig, O jig for me!
My hairt lowps in the breist o me!

Div ye mynd yon officer, Kittie – ?
My dirk he didna 'scape . . .
Div ye mynd him, shyster Kittie?
Your memorie's unco blate!

C'mon, I'll fresh your memorie
When I'm atween the sheets wi ye!

Ye were braw in dou-gray gaiters, then,
And staw'd your gob wi Mignon chocs;
Ye'd officers for your joes, then,
But nou ye've juist the jocks!

Come spreid your hochs for me, hen!
Your saul will feel mair cantie, then!

VI

Aince mair the droshki hurls by,
Fleean, yallan, doun the street . . .
Halt! Halt! Hey, Andra! Here!
And you rin round ahint them, Pate!

Crack-tararack-tak-tak-tak-tak!
The snaw swirls liftward frae the track!
John and the cabbie dash doun the road . . .
We'se gie'm anither round, lads! Load!

Crack-tararack! Maybe yon'll learn ye
To gang wi anither's lass, my bairnie!

Och, the bystart's awa! But nae hairm!
The morn's morn he'se get his fairin!

But whar's my Kittie? – Deid! – She's deid!
Stairk wi a bullet throu her heid!
Weill, Kit, are ye brawlie nou? — Nae word . . .
Ligg there i' the snaw, then! Feed the birds! . . .

Watch your step, my traistie fiere!
The enemie sleeps gey lichtlie here!

VII

Forrart aye the twal men mairchan,
On their shouthers rifles hingan,
But ne'er a gliff o the dowie face
O' the puir laddie 'at murder'd Kate.

Aa the while his pace
Gets quicker and mair quick,
The clout around his craig is taiglit,
He canna set his sel to richts.

Ye're awfae doulie, brither!
Whit gars ye be sae wae, Pate?
Why be sae douncast, Peter?
Is't grievin for your Kate?

Och, guid fieres o mine
I loed the queyne . . .
Nichts wi her I mynd
Mirkie and ree wi wine –
And, for the bricht defyant
Lowe in her een,
And for yon purpie birth-scaur
On her richt shouther,
For thae, like a fule, I shot her,
Ay, in my wuddreme murder'd her. . . .

Ye muckle sumph, are ye greitan, then?
Are ye a lassie, Pate, or a man?
Wad ye like maybe to flype your saul
Insides out, ye glaikit fule?
Haud up your heid! C'mon!
Pull yoursel thegither, man!

Hit's no juist the moment
To nurse ye like a wean!
And there's muckle waur coman,
My auld friend!

And Peter slaws
His borneheid step,
Lifts his heid
And sune cheers up. . . .

> *Hey, jig a jig, O jig for me!*
> *Whit's the crime in a wee bit spree?*

Steek your winnocks, steek your doors –
There's thieves about, my douce neibours!

Unslot your howffs, set up a gless! . . .
There's drouthie tinks in toun, my lass!

VIII

Och, we's wearie-wae!
Dowie and dreich!
Bored til daith!

But I'll fill up the time –
I'll fill it tae hell!

Wi a lassie to daff wi –
I'll daff her tae hell!

70

I'll scart my powe –
I'll scart it tae hell!

And chow my baccy –
I'll chow it tae hell!

And flash my shiv
I'll flash it tae hell!

Flee awa, bourgeois, like wee speugs!
    Or I'se soup your bluid
    For my wee luve's sake
Wi her brous sae black. . . .

Grant peace til Thy servant's saul, O Lord!
    Christ, but I'm bored!

IX

Quaet is aa the citie nou,
Neath Nevski Touer aa is calm,
There's deil the polis in the toun —
Cheer up, fellies! – tho we haena a dram!

The bourgeois stands at the street corner
His neb weill-happit in his collar,
By him a scruntie tyke is standan
Chutteran wi tail dounhingan.

The bourgeois stands like the stairvan tyke,
Stands speakless like a question-mark –
Wi 'ts tail atween its legs, at his back
Stands the auld world, like the hameless tyke.

X

The cavaburd aye rages snell.
    Aye the wind! Aye the snaw!
Tane canna see the tither ava
    Fowr steps awa!

The snaw in a spiral whirls,
The snaw in a spielan column sworls. . . .

71

Jeez, what a storm! . . . O, Christ abune!
– Hey, Pate! Dinna stairt on yon!
What guid's your Christ e'er dune for you?
Ye're an ignorant gett! Is there nae
Reid bluid on your hands, aye weet,
For luve o your Kate?

Revolutionaries, mynd your step!
The enemie's near and doesna sleep!

On! On! On!
Workers o the land!

XI

And, fleeran at the hailie name, they mairch,
 Aa the twal, on and on . . .
 Redd for ocht,
 Dauntit by nocht. . . .

Their steel rifles at the readie
For the enemie unseen
In the tuim and mirkie closes
Whar the blizzard blaws its lane,
The snaw-wreithes sae saft and deep
Your buits're near tint at ilka step. . . .

And waffan at their heid,
 A flag, bluid-reid.
 An echo's heard
 O' a meisur't step.
 . . . Tak tent! . . .
Our enemies never sleep.

And the cavaburd blaws aye in their een
 Nichtlang, daylang,
 Wi nae devall. . . .

On! On! On!
Workers o the land!

72

XII

On, on, they mairch wi solemn pace. . . .
Wha's there? Out wi ye! Out! –
It's nocht but the wind that bangs
Their reid standart about.

Fornent them the cauld snaw-wreithe. . . .
Wha's there? Out wi ye! Out! –
It's nocht but the hameless hungert tyke
Dreichlie hirplan about.

Out the road, ye touzie tyke!
Or I'se kittle your ribs wi my bayonet! —
Auld world, ye touzie tyke,
Be aff, or be stack, ye gett!

He bares his fangs like a faimisht wolf,
His tail hings doun, but he winna muve,
The messan tyke, the chutteran cur –
C'mon nou! Speak! Wha gangs there?

Wha's yonder, wi the Reid Flag! There!
Can ye see the man? It's mirk as hell!
Wha's yonder, rinnan by the houses?
In the shadaws dernan his sel?

Och, never heed — I'se get ye yet!
Surrender, man, for your ain guid!
– Nou then, brither, ye've been tellt!
Come out! – Or we shoot!

Crak-tak-tak! – Nocht but the echo
Dinnles frae ilka house . . .
Nocht but the gowlan cavaburd
Lauchs frae the snaw-wreithe in the close!

> *Crack-tak-tak!*
> *Crack-tak-tak!* . . .

And sae they mairch with sovereign tread . . .
At their heels the stairvan tyke . . .
The bluid-reid standart at their heid . . .
And, skaithless frae their bullets' flicht,
Seen by nane i' the snawblind nicht,
Throu the storm wi lichtlie pace,
Aa besprent wi pearls o ice,
His croun a white nimbus o roses,
Aye at their heid there mairches – Jesus.

Tom Scott

FROM THE GREEK OF SAPPHO

Doun gaes the muin hersel, an aa
The Pleiades forbye.
Nicht is nearin her mirkest hoor
And yet mylane I lie.

FROM THE ITALIAN OF DANTE ALIGHIERI

PAOLO AND FRANCESCO (INFERNO, CANTO 5)

Syne I turnit back ti them and said:
  Francesca, your disaster gars me greit
  Wi doole and petie. Tell me, whit wes't made
While still your love wes biddable and sweet
  (An bi whit snare yir weirdit sauls were taen)
  Love grant ye leave to pree sic taintit meat?
And syne she said: There is nae greater pain
  Than to be myndit o tint happiness
  In misery, as your auld guide suld ken.
But gin ye maun hear whit wey we dree aa this
  For lovin owre unwicely and owre-weill,
  I'll tell ye, tho wi doole, o oor first kiss.
Yae day we read thegither yon auld tale
  O Lancelot and hou he pyned in love.
  We were oorlane, and took nae thocht o ill.
Mony a time my een met his above
  The page, and aa oor pallor turnit reid.
  But yae thing anerlie could oor dounfaa prove.
When, hou that sair-saucht smile wes kissed, we read,
  Bi sic a lover, he, I maun confess
  Wham naethin nou can pairt me frae, tho deid,
Pressit on my mooth a tremlan kiss.
  That book, that author, Galeotto proved.
  We read that day nae farther on nor this . . .
While the ae ghaist telt me hou they loved,
  Tither grat, till I could staund nae mair
  And sank doun in a dwaum, I wes sae moved,
Like a deean man I sprachlet on the fluir.

FROM INFERNO, CANTO 26

Syne, cairryan back and furth, the tap o it
   As gin it were the tongue itsel that spak,
   Bevert furth a voice that uttert: "When
I took my weygaein frae thon Circe, wha
   Near Gaeta, had abuin a year backheld me,
   Lang or Enie gied the place its name,
Neither browdenan on my son, nor thocht
   For my auld faither, nor yet the aucht love
   That should hae made Penelope sae crouse,
Could get the better in me o the yare
   I had for mair experience o life,
   The warld, and ilka human vice and virtue.
Furth I set ance mair upon the swaw
   Wi ae ship but, and thon wee companie
   That hadnae plunkt and left me on mylane.
I saw baith the shores as hyne as Spain
   And as Morocco, and the inch Sardinia,
   And ither isles that thon sea synds around.
Me and my compengons were auld and sweirt
   When, in time, we cam til the nairrae pass
   Whaur Herakles had lang put up his meeths
To hender men frae anterin mair furth.
   On the richt loof, Seville fell ahent,
   And Ceuta on the left wes already gane.
"O brithers", said I, "wha hae throu a hunder
   Thousant dangers raxt the wast wi me,
   Til this last waik, O til this last jimp waik
o whatever senses aye are left til ye,
   Dinna stint yoursels experience o
   The fowkless warld that liggs ahent the sun;
Think ye o your athil race and birth:
   You werenae meant to live as baests maun live,
   You were born to follow truth, and worth."
Wi this short speak I made my companie
   That yare and aiverin for it, that
   Gin I'd seyed, I couldna hae held them back.
And, swingan round my forestem til the greikin,
   Wings we made our oars for the skeery flicht,
   And aye we won guid fordel til the left.
Nicht already saw the ither pole
   Wi aa its starns, and saw ours sae laich
   That frae the ocean fluir it didna ryse.
Five times had kennlet, quelled and kennlet again,
   The eerie licht that leams doun frae the muin,
   Since we had first ingane the fashious wey,

When up kythed a mountain there afore us,
  Blear wi hyneness, and it seemd til me
  The heichest mountain I had ever seen.
We laucht for seil, but suin we laucht bomulloch,
  For frae our new-fund land a storm wes born
  That struck athort the forestem o our ship
And gart her birl three times round wi the swaws,
  And at the fowrth it gart the forestem heeze,
  Syne seg doun in the sea, as wes Their will,
Until the ocean gurled abuin our heids."

FROM THE FRENCH OF FRANÇOIS VILLON

1

BALLAT O THE APPEAL

Whit think ye nou, Garnier, my man,
O my appeal? Ye hoped I'd dee?
Ilka baest saves his ain skin.
Nae maitter hou braw the mews may be,
Gie a bird the chance, and awa he'll flee.
When fowk were aa for haean me hung,
Judged out o hand by swickerie,
Wes yon a time to haud my tongue?

Had I been o King Hughie's line,
The heir o a butcher's dynastie,
Ye'd ne'er swalled me like a sausage-skin
Wi puir man's wine in your surgerie –
Ay, ye ken the gangrel-clek, I see!
When ye were ettlan to hae me flung
Til the gallows-birds by a fell coorse lee,
Wes yon a time to haud my tongue?

D'ye think I staw this heid o mine
Wi no as muckle philosophie
As to raer out "I'm appealan", syne?
Gin that's your thocht, I'm tellan ye
Juist hou faur it gangs ajee.
When I wes telt: "Ye're to be strung
By the haus till daed", man answer me,
Wes yon a time to haud my tongue?

76

Prince, gin I'd played Raw Johnie,
Out there wi Clotaire I'd be swung
Like some hoodie-craw in a poulet-ree!
Wes yon a time to haud my tongue?

2

BALLAT O THE LEDDIES O LANGSYNE

Tell me whaur, in whit countrie
Bides Flora nou, yon Roman belle?
Whaur Thais, Alcibiades be,
Thon sibbit cuisins: can ye tell
Whaur clettaran Echo draws pell-mell
Abuin some burn owrehung wi bine
Her beautie's mair nor human spell –
Ay, whaur are the snaws o langsyne?

Whaur's Heloise, yon wyce abbess
For wham Pete Abelard manless fell,
Yet lovin aye, at Sanct Denys
Wrocht out his days in cloistrit cell?
And say whaur yon queen is as well
That ordrit Buridan ae dine
Be seckt and cuist in the Seine to cool –
Ay, whaur are the snaws o langsyne?

Queen Blanch, as pure's the flouer-de-lys,
Whase voice nae siren's could excel,
Bertha Braid-fuit, Beatrice, Alys,
Ermbourg wha hent the Maine hersel?
Guid Joan of Arc, the lass they tell
The Inglish brunt at Rouen hyne –
Whaur are they, Lady, I appeal?
Ay, whaur are the snaws o langsyne?

Prince, this week I cannae well,
Nor this year, say whaur nou they shine:
Speir, ye'll but hear the owrecome swell –
Ay, whaur are the snaws o langsyne?

77

3

BALLAT O THE HINGIT

Brither-men wha eftir us live on,
Harden no your herts agin us few,
But petie the puir chiels ye gove upon,
And God mair likely your fauts will forhou.
Five or sax o's strung up here ye view,
Our tramorts, doutless pampert yince wi stew,
Theirsels are suppit, tho gey wersh the brew.
When our banes til dust and ashes faa,
Dinna lauch at the sinners dree sic rue,
But pray the Lord hes mercy on us aa.

And gif we caa ye "brethren", dinna scorn
The humble claim, evin tho it's true
It's juist we swing. Weill ye ken nae man born
No aa the time is blessed wi mense enou.
Sae, for our cause, guid-hertit brethren, sue
Wi the Virgin's Son they hingit on Calvarie's bou,
That grace devall afore our juidgment's due
And snek us up in time frae hell's gret maw.
Sen we are deid, ye needna girn at's nou,
But pray the Lord hes mercy on us aa.

We hae been washed and purifee'd by rain.
The sun hes tanned our hides a leathery hue.
Craws and pyes hae pykit out our een,
And barbered ilka stibble-chin and brou.
Nae peace we ken the twenty-fowr hours throu,
For back and furth, whiles braid-on, whiles askew,
Wi ilka wind that blaws we twist and slue;
Mair stoggit nor straeberries, and juist as raw.
See til it *ye* never mell wi sic a crew,
And pray the Lord shaws mercy til us aa.

Prince Jesus, wha haud aa mankind in feu,
Watch Satan duisna reive us serfs frae you;
Wi him we'll byde nae langer nor we awe.
Guid-fellae-men, dinnae ye mock us nou,
But pray the Lord shaws mercy til us aa.

FROM THE FRENCH OF CHARLES BAUDELAIRE

GLOAMIN

Comes the gloamin hour, the cut-throat's freend;
Comes on sleekit fuit wi wowfish mien.
The lift like an auditorium dims doun,
And Man waits till his change til baest comes round.

O Nicht! O freendly Nicht, fair dear til men
Whase airms and harns can say: "This day, Guid kens,
We've duin our darg!" The nicht alane can cure
The faroush pain in eident spriets and dour –
The trauchlet scholar's, as he rubs his brou;
The forfairn workman's, hapt in the bed-clathes nou.

Bylins, the air's malorous deils again
Sweirtlie steir theirsels like business-men
To jow, in their flicht, the gable-ends and shutters.
Frae their red lamps the wind shaks owre the gutters,
Like some ant-hill that opens wide its doors,
Streets are lichtit by the sauls o whures;
Like traitors, aye some dernlike wey they shaw
Til chiels wha kill guid-livin at a blaw;
They steir the glaur o ilka toun's main street
Like scoyan worms fowk dinnae ken they eat.

Here and there, ye smell a kitchen's brew,
Hear theatres roar, some band channer and mew.
Mirklan cafés, spivs' haunts and their ilk,
Fill up wi pimps, and whures in crepe and silk,
And picklocks, saikless o guid sense or thocht,
Cantilie gang til the ae darg they're aucht,
Cannilie forsean windae, safe and lock,
For daily breid – and to cled some doxie's dock.

Steel yoursel in this mirk nicht, my saul!
Turn a deif ear til yon caiterwaul.
This is the hour when seikly fowk get waur.
The mirk nicht grips them by the throat, and owre
They gang, intil the pit whaur they began:
The wards are fu o their sichin – mair nor ane
Willnae come back to prieve the Sunday jynt
By the fire, nor clek wi cronies owre a pint.

Ay, maist o them hae never kent a hame,
Nor muckle else in life, forbye their name.

William J. Tait

FROM THE FRENCH OF FRANÇOIS VILLON

ON DAETH

Muild-rich or puir, I ken ower weel,
Wise-haid an witless, laird an loon,
Fair an ill-fettered, fause an leal,
Wi plooman's duds or preacher's goon;
An wear dey hap or wear dey croon,
Leddy an limmer, tink an queen,
Wi hair piled hych or hingin doon,
Da haund o Daeth yocks every een.

Sood Paris fair or Helen dee,
Wha-ever dees, dees wi a stang
At smores his frychtened sauchs an wi
Gaa brackin trow his hert an crang.
He swaets . . . God kens whit rivin pang
Bracks his daeth-swaet, for nane can aise
His toarments, nor, his kin amang,
Wid wife or bairn tak his dreed place.

Daeth drains da bluid fae his cauld face;
Trow his stret haase da black veins shaw;
His hench-joints sturken stiff in place;
His flesh faas slack an slouchs awa.
O lovely limbs an breests laek snaw,
Smooth, satin-saft, a keeng wid prize!
Man Beauty's sel sic ills befaa?
Yea, or geng livin ta da skies!

FROM THE FRENCH OF PIERRE DE RONSARD

SONNET FOR HELEN

Some nycht whin du is aald an, glansin on da brace,
Da caandle lychts dy wheel, weel set in ta da fire,
Noenin my sangs, du'll hark: "Whin I wis eence da vyre
O aa da laand, Ronsard, due roessed my boannie face."

Dan no a servant lass at neebs ower her hap-lace
An dovers ower oot-doen wi darg o hoose an byre,
Bit, whin shu hears my name, her haand 'ill slip da wire
An rise as if ta bliss dee, daethliss by my grace.

Toh under fael my banes in some aeth-kent kirkyaird,
Amang da mychty skalds A'll tak my aise at last.
Ower da hertstane du'll cooir, failed, craapen, nigh twa-faald,

An graim ower my lost love an dy prood disregaird.
Live, if du'll ent me noo: waitna till du's grown aald.
Gadder Life's flooers afore dy day an dirs is past.

FROM THE DANISH OF MARTIN MELSTED

DA DRAEMIN SKALD

Tae Marc Chagall

In Vitebsk da fock waitit
An baigit an gret
An dir prayer wis da lyood
Fae da ferrie fiddlers' knowe
An da midders' saat tairs
Goed rowin in straems
Oot ta da faar haaf
Whaar de maalie loems mirrored
Da lily an rose
An oot an in da hooses
Goed da nycht's moen an staars
An da moarn's sun gloored raid
I da cock's kame on da toonmals.

Da lass du loves burns wi a lowe
Laek dy bridal nycht caandle
An lychts aa da rod trow da toon
Whaar da wind noens its fey sang
Tae Revolution's dowd and feddit flags.
Dy lass lowes laek da fire.

Dy love waits dee nakit
I da tree's green laives
An wants dee ta come
An draim her a horse
An a coo an a hoose
An draim at Belsen-berge
Is aunly a wanrestit draim.

Sae you baith waander doon ta da moedoo
Anunder da mirknin trees
Laek corbies' wings doon-laavin
Laek da slycht mirk faa o dy draimin lass's hair.
Sae you lay you doon dare an pictir
Your ain world o fock an baess
While da fires o Auschwitz ir slockin
In yallow daala-reek.

Blinnd waanders Goad ower da Aert
A poor aald country fiddler
At canna mak oot da hoose again
Whaar da streen dey gae him maet.
Sin du meets him, will du len him
Dy draimin een, Chagall?
Sae at Goad can see his toonship
An kain his twa lovers agaen;
Sae at fiddle strings can link at
Dir glansin laivrick sang
An da sun staand still in Lebanon
An da muin ower Geedeon's daal.

FROM THE FRENCH OF GEORGES BRASSENS

AN ILL NAME

Ida toonship at I caa hame
A'm gotten somewy an ill name.
Whidder I dance or whidder I sit,
A'm taen for I-kenna-whit.
Wrang, bi my will, I never did ta nonn,
As I traivel in pace my ain rod hom'.
Bit da braa sheelds is whick ta blem,
If ye tak a different gait fae dem.
Aa da world spaeks ill o me –
Aa bit da dumb fock, dat you'll see!

On Up Helly Aa nycht, snug I lay
Soond asleep i my seck o hey.
Da skirlin pipes at goed dirlin by
Hed naethin ta doe wi me, tocht I.
Wrang, bi my will, I never did ta nonn,
Toh I never heard da euphonium gronn.
Bit de braa sheelds is whick ta blem,
If ye tak a different gait fae dem.
Aabody points da finger at me —
Aa bit da haandless, dat you'll see!

An ill-luckit tief tries ta nick a fry
An a Burraman soinds him . . . Whit doe I?
I stick oot a fit, an – I doe declare! –
Da Burraman ends up erse i da air!
Wrang, bi my will, I never did ta nonn,
Littin some peerie whinsie mak a run.
Bit da braa sheelds is whick ta blem,
If ye tak a different gait fae dem.
Aa da world 'ill buck ower me –
Aa bit da legless, dat you'll see!

Jeremiah dir nae need ta be
Ta spo whit fate's in store for me.
'S shoen's dey fin a rop at dey laek,
D'ill hae 'im dranged aboot my neck.
Wrang, bi my will, I never did ta nonn,
Traivlin ony rod at dusna laid to Rom'.
Bit da braa sheelds is whick ta blem,
If ye tak a different gait fae dem.
Aabody 'ill come ta see me hanged –
Aa bit da sychtless, bi my sang!

Hamish Henderson

FROM THE GREEK OF C. P. CAVAFY

TOMB OF IASES

Iases lies here. In this city of cities
A boy renowned for his grace and beauty.
Scholars admired me, and also the people –
The rough and the ready.
                    To all sorts I gave pleasure.

But because the world thought me Narcissus
    and Hermes,
Abuses consumed me and killed me.
                            Passer-by,
If you are from Alexandria, you will not
    blame me.
You know the fury, the pace of our life here –
What ardour there is, what extreme pleasure.

FROM THE ITALIAN OF DINO CAMPANA

CHIMAERA

Ignorant whether your pale face
appeared to me among rocks,
or if you were
a smile from unknown distances,
your bent ivory forehead gleaming,
young sister of the Gioconda:
or whether you were
the smile of extinguished springtimes,
mythical in your paleness,
O Queen, Queen of our adolescence:
but for your unknown poem
of voluptuousness and grief
marked by a line of blood
in the circle of your sinuous lips,
musical bloodless girl,
Queen of melody:
but for your virginal head
reclined, I, poet of the night,
kept vigil over the bright stars
in the oceans of the sky;

I, for your tender mystery,
I, for your silent blossoming.
Ignorant whether the pale fire
of your hair was the living
mark of your paleness,
or was a gentle vapour
drifting over my pain,
the smile of a face by night alone.
I gaze on the white rocks, the
   silent sources of the winds,
and the immobility of the firmament,
and the swollen rivers that flow
   lamenting
and the shadow of human labour
   stooped over the cold hills,
and again through limpid skies towards
   far-off free-coursing shadows
again
      and yet again
           I call you
             Chimaera

FROM THE ITALIAN OF ALFONSO GATTO

O H, the faded churches in the fields,
the channels of the grass where the wind
climbs the steps, carrying its silences
and the wooden doors, and the tinkling
of a bell, up to the iron gates. . . .
But the country will go down into the sea
to find its dead, the bare ironworks
of the world and in the houses the vast
silence of the crosses. Like marble
that love will be cold which burns more fiercely
with the remaining lights and the shouting –
deep down, deep down in our black blood.
Naked that day it will break through
into the thick of the thighs of snow.
The coral on the red mouth will drown
in darkness, and the lights extinguish
its songs against a background
of rainwet nights. . . .
the sea the sea will hurl on to the long
dreams the rains and the hovels, carrying the vast
odour of the earth and the tombs.

Edwin Morgan

FROM THE ITALIAN OF FRANCESCO PETRARCA

SONNETS

1

The eyes that drew from me such fervent praise,
the arms and hands and feet and countenance
which made me a stranger in my own romance
and set me apart from the well-trodden ways;

the gleaming golden curly hair, the rays
flashing from a smiling angel's glance
which moved the world in paradisal dance,
are grains of dust no passion now can raise.

And I live on, but in grief and self-contempt,
left here without the light I loved so much,
in a great tempest and with shrouds unkempt.

No more love songs, then, I have done with such;
my old skill now runs thin at each attempt,
and tears are heard within the harp I touch.

2

The woods are wild and were not made for man.
Now men and weapons fill them with their fear.
I walk there free, the only terror near
being my Sun and the bright rays I scan –

her piercing Love! And I walk singing (but can
such thoughts be wise?) of her who in absence is here,
here in my eyes and heart to make me swear
I saw girls, ladies, where beech and fir trees ran!

I seem to hear her, when I hear the air,
the leaves, the branches, the complaint of birds,
or waters murmuring on through the green grass.

Never so happy, never in silence so rare,
alone in a grim forest, without light, without words –
but still too far out from my Sun I pass!

LOVE LYRICS

1

Suddenly dazzled by lighting in the fields
a man sees instant darkness everywhere;
then when the gradual brightness reappears
he guards his eyes against the fires of the air.
　　But I, in safety perfectly instructed
by flash of your inimitable grace
which threw in shadow every joy I had had
with those most sweet yet sharply-showered rays,
no longer err in plain and daily light.
　　For now to adore you is my light and life.

2

To speak, or not, no man will disallow
who gives the rein of freedom to the will.
Yet, should it happen someone says to you,
Lady, either your lover lies forgetful
or else he draws his Délie from the moon
to show you at evasive wax and wane –
let that execrable name depart
from you to him who angles for our hurt!
　　In that admirable name I would conceal
you, shining in the dark night of my soul.

SONNETS

1

One moment my hope rises up on wings,
the next, grown weary of its high estate,
it turns and falls, and leaves me, like my fate,
wide open to the diffidence it brings.
   What man would bear such harsh revisitings
of evil to good? O wearied heart, be great!
Make strength in misery your surrogate;
waits for the calms that follow buffetings.
   And I myself will promise by main force
to break obstructions none have dared to break,
bristling with thousands of impediments.
   No death or stumbling-blocks or prison-doors
can keep you from my sight, though they should make
my naked ghost gaze through its fleshy rents.

2

While there is still the colour of a rose
and of a lily in your countenance,
and you with such an ardent candid glance
can fire the heart, and check the flames it shows;
   and while that golden hair of yours that flows
into a knot can leap into a dance
as the wind blows with livelier dalliance
upon the fairest proud white neck it knows:
   gather together from your happy spring
fruits that are sweet, before time ravages
with angry snow the beauty of your head.
   The rose will wither as the cold wind rages,
and age come gently to change everything,
lest our desire should change old age instead.

3

I came to a valley in the wilderness
where no one walked across the waste but me,
and there I saw a sudden misery,
a dog, distraught, wild with unhappiness.

Its howl would mount into the emptiness,
and then it would go sniffing eagerly
for tracks, run on, turn back, and stop – to be
fretted again by a desperate distress.
    And it was this: the dog had missed the presence
of its master; could not find him; felt its loss.
See what straits they drive to, the ills of absence!
    The dog's bewilderment tore my heart across;
I said to it in pity: "Cling to patience:
I am a man, yet absence is my cross."

FROM THE ITALIAN OF TORQUATO TASSO

LOVE LYRICS

1

To what joys could I aspire
when I am so far from you who are all my desire?
And yet by sleight of mind
I cross the hills and fields and streams and seas
to be near you again and find
my heart blaze up in the light of your eyes, and be pleased
by the very pain that is kind
for one who is infinitely happy to die in that fire.

2

So far from you, my dear!
I have no heart, no life; Tasso is not here.
No more, alas, no more
what I once was, but a piece of darkness, a shade,
a sound like the sound of pain,
a desolation, a voice: and this is nothing more
than what your absence has made;
I still have a mortal sickness – if death was near!

3

No flowers by these shores
bear such a lovely red
as the red that blooms along the lips of my love,
and no air that blows
in June by the lily-bed
or by river and rose has a song as sweet to sing of.
Ah may I only miss
the music of those dear lips in the pause of a kiss!

4

Most perfect kiss –
this softest recompense
for serving you with my tireless faithfulness!
and O most happy hand
that trembles like a bird
and yet is bold to touch your gentle breast,
while sweetness has entranced
the soul that seals our lips to swoon to its rest!

5

What were the dews I saw,
the lamentations or the tears
scattered abroad from under the cowl and shawl
of night, from the sweet white face of the stars?
And why did the snowy moon throw and strew
so pure a shower of sparkling drops across
the fresh and glistening grass?
Why were the winds that blew
through the dark air before daybreak so bleak,
wheeling and wailing as in grief?
Shall I say they are all witnesses, when you depart,
dear heart of my heart?

6

Silent the forests, the streams,
waveless-sheeted the sea,
winds in their caves unblustering, at peace,
sombre the night, and white
its moon of deepest and marmoreal quiet:
let us too lie like secrets
locked in love and its sweetness –
love have no breath, no voice,
no sound a kiss, no voice or sound my sighs!

FROM THE ITALIAN OF GIAMBATTISTA MARINO

LOVE LYRICS

1

My hidden treasure is love
and my heart is its treasurer;
may he lock up my longings there!
And O my sighs, mysterious witnesses
of the love I steal, voices
that my lips are parted to utter again and again –
keep your silence before men,
for this, alas, all schools of love can teach:
a sigh in itself is speech.

2

That pair of gleaming snakes,
twisted into little orbs of enamel and gold,
which your lovely ear shakes,
Lilla, as pendants: they hold
some message, don't they? Yes, yes, I know:
these are the mysterious insignia of others'
pain, cruel, gratuitous;
like a biting snake you go
cruelly wounding others, your deaf ear takes
no prayers, tears, heartbreaks.

FROM THE RUSSIAN OF ALEXANDER PUSHKIN

AUTUMN

1

October has come – already now the wood
Casts its last leaves, its branches are all bare;
Autumn has breathed its cold to freeze the road,
Beyond the mill the stream still murmurs there,
But the pond's already ice; my neighbour's load
Of hunting-hounds is shot off with wild blare
To ravage winter crops in distant fields;
They bay until the sleeping forest yields.

2

Now is my time: I hold no brief for spring;
Tiresome thaw with its slush and stench – I'm ill
In spring, blood fevered, mind and heart panting
With longing. Rough-hewn winter meets the bill
Far better; I love its snows; our sledge stealing
Through moonlight, swift, at its own airy will,
While a warm hand stirs from beneath her sable
To press my hand, and make her flush and tremble!

3

What a delight to glide on sharp-shod iron
Across the smooth unruffled river-glass!
Winter festivals all shimmer and fire! . . .
But snow for six months? No, I think I'll pass:
Even for bears in dens it might be fine
At first, but not at last. You can't amass
Pleasure for ever from Juliet in a sledge,
Or vegetate by stove and window-ledge.

4

Summer, you beauty! I would be truly yours
But for the heat and dust, the midges and the flies.
You drain our mental strength, and what tortures
You give us! Like the field, the body cries
For rain; to be where drink and freshness pours;
Only to see old mother winter rise
Once more: pancakes and wine for her farewell,
Ice and ice-cream for her memorial.

5

Late autumn days are no one's favourite,
And yet, you know, I find this season dear.
Its still beauty, its shining placid spirit
Attract me like a Cinderella's tear.
I tell you frankly I can see no merit
In any other season of the year.
Such good, in autumn? Yes, I can discover
Its beckoning essence, and I am no boastful lover.

6

How to persuade you? Were you ever taken
By some unrobust girl wasting away –
Strange, but it's like that. She is stricken,
Death-bent, poor creature, unrepining prey
Of unseen jaws whose grip will never slacken;
She smiles still, with red lips that fade to grey;
Her face has twilight in its blood, not dawn;
Alive today, tomorrow she is gone.

7

Melancholy time, yet magic to the sight!
Leavetaking kinds of beauty please me best:
All nature withering in a sumptuous light,
The groves and forests gold-and-purple-dressed,
The wind-loud tree-crests, the airy delight,
The mists that roll to trouble the sky's rest,
The rare sun-ray and the first test of frost,
The distant menace of winter's grizzled ghost.

8

And with each autumn I bud and bloom once more;
The Russian cold is good and therapeutic;
The everyday routines no longer bore:
Hunger and sleep come sweetly automatic;
Joy dances lightly where my heart's tides pour,
Desire swirls up – I'm young again, an addict
Of life and happiness – that's my organism
(And please forgive this forced prosaicism.)

9

My horse is brought; it shakes its mane and takes
Its rider out into the wilderness,
The frostbound glen where every hoofbeat strikes
Flashes, rings loud, while ice cracks in the stress.
But the short day goes grey, and the fire-flakes
Play up in the forgotten grate, now less,
Now more, now smouldering and now flaring:
I read there, or I feed my long thoughts, staring.

10

And I forget the world – and in dear silence
Am dearly lulled by my imagination,
And poetry wakens into consciousness:
My soul is rocked in lyric agitation,
It cries and trembles, and like a dreamer frets
To free itself in full manifestation –
And now a swarm of unseen guests draws near,
Both old friends and imagined shapes are here.

11

And brave thoughts break like waves along my brain,
And rhymes race forward to the rendezvous,
And pen beckons to finger, paper to pen.
One minute, and verse surges freely through.
So a stilled ship drowses on the stilled main,
Till look: a sudden leaping of the crew,
Masts are shinned up and down, sails belly free,
The huge mass moves and slices through the sea.

12

Great to sail off with it! But where to go?
What lands shall we now see: vast Caucasus,
Or some sun-blistered Moldavian meadow,
Or Normandy's snow-gleaming policies,
Or Switzers' pyramid array on show,
Or wild and sad Scottish rock-fortresses . . . ?

NOTE

The unfinished twelfth stanza occurs only in a rough draft in
Pushkin's autograph.

FROM THE RUSSIAN OF VLADIMIR MAYAKOVSKY

1

THE BALLAD O THE RID CADIE

Wance upon a time there lived a Cadet laddie.
And this Cadet laddie had a wee rid cadie.

Forby this bit cadie he'd colleckit fae somebody
the Cadet had fient a rid corpuscle in his body.

He thocht he heard a revo – wheesht though – LUTION, rid
  and bluidy!
The wee Cadet was ready wi his bluid-rid cadie.

Like grumphies in claver lived the haill Cadet caboodle,
the Cadet and his cadaddy and his grampacadoodle.

But up whupt a rouchlin outstrapolous blad o
wind and rippit thon cadie to a shadda.

Cadieless Cadet, black-heidit and shoddy!
The rid wowfs cam and had him wi their toddy.

Aabody kens thae wowfs was no ill-deedie!
But they gowpt him cuffs an aa, like maws at a haddie.

Sae, gin ye pley at politics, my laddie and my leddy,
mind o the ballad o the wee rid cadie.

2

A RICHT RESPECK FOR CUDDIES

Horse-cluifs clantert
giein their patter:
crippity
crappity
croupity
crunt.

Bleezed in the blafferts,
wi ice-shoggly bauchles,
the street birled and stachert.
The cuddy cam clunk,
cloitit doon doup-scud,
and wheech
but the muckle-mou'd moochers werna lang
in makin theirsels thrang,
gawpus eftir gawpus, aa gaw-hawin
alang the Kuznetsky in their bell-bottom breeks.
"Aw, see the cuddy's doon!"
"Aw, it's doon, see the cuddy!"
And aa Kuznetsky gaffit.
Aa but me.
I didna jyne the collieshangie.
I cam and kest
a gliff intil
the cuddy's ee . . .

The street's owrewhammelt
in its ain breenges . . .

I cam and I saw
the muckle draps that scrammelt
doon the cratur's niz-bit
to coorie in its haffits . . .

And oh but the haill
clamjamfry o craturly
cares cam spillin and splairgein
fae my hert wi a reeshle!
"Ned, Ned, dinna greet!
Listen to me, Ned –
ye think thae buggers are the saut o the erd?

My chiel,
neds are we aa, to be honest wi ye;
nae man's unnedlike, in his ain wey."
Aweel, it micht be
the beast was an auld yin
and had nae need o a fyke like me,
or was my thochts a wheen coorse for a cuddy?
Onywey
Ned
gied a loup whaur he liggit,
stoitert to his feet,
gied a nicher
and the flisk
o his tail doon the street.
My chestnut chiel!
Back hame to his stable
lauchin like a pownie
staunin by the stable-waa
feelin in his banes able
to dree the darg and the dowie
for the life that's worth it aa.

3

MAYAKONFERENSKY'S ANECTIDOTE

Nicht haurdly gane: day loups up:
and ilka morn loup wi't
folk to CENTGEN
folk to GENCOM
folk to COMPOLIT
folk to POLITCENT –
hooses skail, offices fill,
till wow! the papers rin like watter,
and if ye seek some matter –
tak hauf a hunnert –
aye, the maist important! –
the boys wi the pens are gane like whittricks
to committees and cognostins and burroos and statistics.

It is mysel:
"Can I no hae an interview, an audition?
The name on the knock's Tammas Fugit, ye ken – "
"Comrade Ivan 'vanich is at a session
of the Union of KINPROP and KULTADMIN."
I stummle up a hunner sterrs.
The licht's kinna dim.
Yince mair:
"They say, come back in an hour.
They are all in session, in conference:
subject, purchase of ink-bottles from
GOVCENTCOOP-ink-bottle-shop."

Eftir an oor –
fient a scriever-chiel,
fient a scriever-lassie –
juist hee-haw.
Ablow 22, they're aa
awa to a session o the KOMSOMO'.

Up I sclim till the nicht's abune me,
tapmaist storey, tapmaist o seeven.
"Can I no see Comrade Ivan 'vanich noo?"
"No, not even
now. In session, in conference, on committee
A and B and C and D and E and F and G and H. Pity!"

Fair scunnert,
in on their sederunt
I breenge like an avalanche, disparplin
my fremit aiths on ilka haun,
when glowff! –
folk cut in hauf, sittin aroon –
bluidy cantrips o auld Mahoun!
And whaur, whaur's their ither hauf?
"It's the slashers!
They're deid!"
I'm ramfeezelt noo, I rair and I bawl,
I'm no concos-mancos wi that grugous sicht.
But a wee wee voice, a wee prignickity
voice o a scriever-cum-key-skelper: "All
the people you see are at *two* conferences; indeed,
they have daily
to attend twenty;
and thus, willy-nilly,
and quite literally,
they must tear themselves apart to appear.

Boots to belt – elsewhere.
Belt and above – in here."

I canny sleep for waumlin thochts.
Nicht's haurdly gane.
Day loups. I see't aa plain:
"Oh for
yin mair
sederunt to convene
to congree to conclude
to comblasticastraflocate sans avizandum
ilka sederunt and tap-table-tandem!"

4

BROOKLYN BRIG

Coolidge ahoy!
Can ye shout wi joy?
This makar'll no be blate
                          at namin
what's guid.
                Blush rid
                          at my praises, you s-
uperunited states-man –
                          rid
                                as the flamin
flag o Sovetsky Soyuz.
Like a cracked sanct
                    hirplin
                          to his kirk,
to some stere,
                semple
                          Culdee wig-
wam o stane,
                here
                        in the grey dwam and mirk
o gloamin
                I set fit doucely on Brooklyn Brig.
Like a conqueror
                enterin
                          the toon he has taen,

99

the swanky
            ridin his cannon-rig
its giraffe-snoot cockit,
                        I'm fu wi glory, I'm fain
o life,
        I'm prood
                    to sclim on Brooklyn Brig.
Like a daft penter-chiel
                        that digs an auld-maister's
madonna wi his sherp lovin een,
                                I trig-
ger my sicht
            fae the airy
                        starn-thrangsters
doon
        through aa New York
                        by Brooklyn Brig.
New York,
            pechin
                    in daylang ure and stour,
pits by
        its trauchle noo,
                        and its giddy waas
shaw nane but freenly spooks
                            that skoor
the lichtit windaes
                    wi hamely-glintin claws.
Ye can juist hear
                the grummle
                            o the rummlin El,
and up here
            there's naethin
                            bar that laich grummle
to tell
        hoo trains
                    are traipsin, clatterin fell,
like ashets in a press
                        flung thegither in a tummle.
See the shopkeeper
                    humphin his sugar fae
a mill
        that seems
                    to loup oot o the stream –
while
        masts gang furrit unner the brae

o the brig
          nae langer nor preens.
It's prood I am
            o this
                 wan mile o steel,
my veesions here
                tak vive and forcy form –
a fecht
       for construction
                 abune flims o style,
a strang
      trig-rivetit grid,
                    juist whit steel's for!
And if
      the feenish o the warld
                    sud come
and chaos
      clout the planet
                 to smithereens
and the wan thing
             left staunin
                 in the sun
sud be this brig spreedeaglt owre the reeky stanes –
then,
     as a hantle
              o puir peerie banes
swalls
     to a curator's
                vaudy dinosaur-chaumer,
sae
   fae this brig
            some faur-aff geologist yonner
in the centuries'll
            bigg up
                the haill warld o oor days.
He'll say:
     "See thon
             muckle steely paw –
it jyned
      the prairies to the seas; fae this end
Europe
      breenged Westwart, Westwart,
                     blawin
a flaff
     o Indian fedders
             doon the wind.

See
    the rib therr –
           minds me o a machine;
I wunner
      staunin wi a steel-fit grup
in Manhattan,
        wid the hauns rax
              steeve and clean
to hook and rug owre
          Brooklyn
             by the lip?
And see
      the electric cable-strands – we ken
it's eftir
      the James Watt era
          that here
the radio
      hud fouth
         o bummin
           men;
and planes
       were fleein
         through
           the atmosphere.
Here,
    some folk
        fund life
           a gairden-pairty,
ithers
    a lang-drawn
        tuim-wame
           granin-time.
Doon therr,
      the workless pairted
fae it,
    heid first
        into the Hudson's slime.
And noo . . .
       noo the eemage
          gaes sae clear, sae faur
it skimmers on the cable-strings
           richt to the feet o the starns.
Here in my een
       I can see
         Mayakovsky staun –
he stauns as a makar,
      the syllables jow in his harns – "

– And I'm gawpin still
                    like an Eskimo at an injin,
like a cleg at the neck-band
                        drinkin it aa in.
Brooklyn Brig –
man . . .
      that's BIG!

FROM THE ITALIAN OF EUGENIO MONTALE

WIND IN THE CRESCENT

The muckle brig didna gang your wey.
Gin ye'd've gien the word, I'd have won through
to ye by navigatin stanks and syvers. But
aa my virr, wi thon sun on the winnocks
o the verandas, wis seepin slawly awa.

A birkie that wis preachin on the Crescent
speirit at me: "D'ye ken whaur Gode is?" I kent
and tellt him. He shook his heid. I saw nae mair
o him in the wud wind that skelpit hooses and fowk
and gart them flee abune the taurry daurk.

FROM THE GERMAN OF BERTOLT BRECHT

1

THE PLUM-TREE

The back-yard has a tiny plum-tree,
it shows how small a tree can be.
Yet there it is, railed round
so no one tramps it to the ground.

It's reached its full shape, low and meagre.
O yes it wants to grow more, it's eager
for what can't be done –
it gets too little sun.

A plum-tree no hand's ever been at
to pick a plum: it strains belief.
It is a plum-tree for all that –
we know it by the leaf.

2

ON WATERING THE GARDEN

O watering of the garden, to put the green in good heart!
Spraying of thirsty trees! Give more than enough and
never forget the shrubbery, not even
the shrub without berries, the exhausted
niggardly bearers. And don't overlook
the weed between the flowers, it too
knows thirst. Nor should you pour
only on the fresh turf or only on the parched turf:
you must refresh the naked earth itself.

3

THE LANDSCAPE OF EXILE

And yet I too, on that last boat,
watched the same cheerful dawn glow through the rigging
and the greyish skins of the dolphins riding
through the Sea of Japan.

The little gilded horse-drawn carts
and the rosy veils on the matrons' arms
in the alleys of Manila, that marked place:
these the fugitive rejoiced to see.

By the high oil derricks and thirsty gardens of Los Angeles
and the twilight gorges of California and its fruit-markets
the bearer of bad luck
was not left cold.

4

A WORKER READS, AND ASKS THESE QUESTIONS

Who built Thebes with its seven gates?
In all the books it says kings.
Did kings drag up those rocks from the quarry?
And Babylon, overthrown time after time,
who built it up again as often? What walls
in dazzling gilded Lima housed the builders?

When evening fell on the completed Wall of China,
where did the stonemasons go? Great Rome
is thick with triumphal arches. Who erected them? Who was it
the Caesars triumphed over? Had famous Byzantium
nothing but palaces, where did people live? Atlantis itself,
that legendary night the sea devoured it, heard
the drowning roaring for their slaves.

The young Alexander took India.
By himself?
Caesar hammered Gaul.
Had he not even a cook beside him?
Philip of Spain cried as his fleet
foundered. Did no one else cry?
Frederick the Second won the Seven Years War. Who
won it with him?

Someone wins on every page.
Who cooked the winners' banquet?
One great man every ten years.
Who paid the expenses?

So many statements.
So many questions.

FROM THE SPANISH OF FEDERICO GARCÍA LORCA

1

SLEEPLESS CITY

(Brooklyn Bridge Nocturne)

No one sleeps in the sky. No one, no one.
No one sleeps.
The moon's creatures prowl and sniff round their cabins.
Living iguanas arrive to gnaw the insomniacs
and the heartbroken man on the run will meet at streetcorners
the quiet incredible crocodile beneath the soft protest of the stars.

No one sleeps in the world. No one, no one.
No one sleeps.
There is a dead man in the farthest-off graveyard
who for three querulous years
has grumbled at the shrivelled landscape fixed to his knees;
and the boy they buried this morning cried so much
they had to call out dogs to give him his quietus.

Life is no dream. Watch out! Watch out! Watch out!
We fall downstairs to eat damp earth
or climb to the snowline with a dead dahlia chorus.
But there is no oblivion, no dream, only
living flesh. Kisses bind mouths
in a maze of fresh veins
and the one whose pain vexes him will be vexed without rest
and the one whom death terrifies will be bowed under it.

One day
horses will neigh in taverns
and rabid ants
will attack the yellow skies lurking in cows' eyes.

Another day
we shall see a resurrection of dissected butterflies
and then as we stroll through a sponge-grey boat-still scene
we shall see our rings flash and our tongues spill roses.

Watch out! Watch out! Watch out!
For those who still guard the claw-tracks and the cloudburst,
that boy weeping because the invention of the bridge is beyond him
or that dead man left with a head and a shoe,
they are all to be taken to the wall where iguanas and snakes are
    waiting,
where the bear's teeth are waiting,
where the mummified hand of the child is waiting
and the camel-skin bristles and shivers in raw blue fever.

No one sleeps in the sky. No one, no one.
No one sleeps.
But if any eye should shut –
lash him awake, boys, lash him!
Imagine a panorama of staring eyes
and bitter sores kept flaming.
No one sleeps in the world. No one, no one.
No one sleeps.
I say it here.
No one sleeps.
But if anyone should find a glut of night moss on his temples –
open the trapdoors and let the moon look down on
the sham wineglasses, the poison, and the skull of the theatres.

2

CASIDA OF WEEPING

My balcony I've drawn, I've shut it –
who could bear to hear this weeping?
And yet the grey walls cannot hide it –
there's no sound but the sound of weeping.

Singing angels are few, are few –
barking dogs are few, are few –
hundreds of violins in the shadow of a hand —

and yet the weeping is a vast dog,
and the weeping is angel and violin,
vast the angel and vast the violin,
the wind is choked with the crying, leaving
no sound but the sound of weeping.

3

CASIDA OF THE DARK DOVES

It was through the laurel boughs
I saw the two dark doves.
One dove was the sun
and the other was the moon.
"Where, little neighbours, where
is my tomb, is it there or here?"
"Tomb in my tail" (said the sun).
"Tomb in my throat" (said the moon).
And I, as I still travelled
with the living earth at my belt
saw the two eagles of snow
and a girl naked as day.
One eagle was the other
and the naked girl was neither.
"Where, little eagles, where
is my tomb, is it there or here?"
"Tomb in my throat" (said the sun).
"Tomb in my throat" (said the moon).
It was through the laurel boughs
I saw two naked doves.
One dove was the other
and the two doves were neither.

4

Song of the Little Death

Lawns of the leprous moons
and blood at the heart of the world.
Lawns of inveterate blood.

Light of days gone and to come.
Skies of the leprous grass.
Light and darkness of sand.

I found myself with death.
Lawns of the leprous earth.
A little thing was death.

The dog above in the eaves.
My left and lonely hand
crossed a great tableland
of flowers dry as leaves.

Cathedral made of ashes.
Light and darkness of sand.
A little death for man.

A death and I a man.
A man alone, and it
a little death, so little –

Lawns of the leprous moons.
The snow shudders and moans
on the far side of the door.

A man: what more? As before –
it, and that lonely man.
Lawns, love, light, and sand.

FROM THE HUNGARIAN OF SÁNDOR WEÖRES

1

ETERNAL MOMENT

What you don't trust to stone
and decay, shape out of air.
A moment leaning out of time
arrives here and there,

guards what time squanders, keeps
the treasure tight in its grasp –
eternity itself, held
between the future and the past.

As a bather's thigh is brushed
by skimming fish – so
there are times when God
is in you, and you know:

half-remembered now
and later, like a dream.
And with a taste of eternity
this side of the tomb.

2

MONKEYLAND

Oh for far-off monkeyland,
ripe monkeybread on baobabs,
and the wind strums out monkeytunes
from monkeywindow monkeybars.

Monkeyheroes rise and fight
in monkeyfield and monkeysquare,
and monkeysanatoriums
have monkeypatients crying there.

Monkeygirl monkeytaught
masters monkeyalphabet,
evil monkey pounds his thrawn
feet in monkeyprison yet.

Monkeymill is nearly made,
miles of monkeymayonnaise,
winningly unwinnable
winning monkeymind wins praise.

Monkeyking on monkeypole
harangues the crowd in monkeytongue,
monkeyheaven comes to some,
monkeyhell for those undone.

Macaque, gorilla, chimpanzee,
baboon, orangutan, each beast
reads his monkeynewssheet at
the end of each twilight repast.

With monkeysupper memories
the monkeyouthouse rumbles, hums,
monkeyswaddies start to march,
right turn, left turn, shoulder arms –

monkeymilitary fright
reflected in each monkeyface,
with monkeygun in monkeyfist
the monkeys' world the world we face.

FROM THE RUSSIAN OF GENNADY AIGI

1

ONCE MORE: PLACES IN THE FOREST

again *they are being sung*! they are! again *they*
are resounding — everywhere – in unison! —

again about that time
wakening-time:

brightly
– by-the-meadow-of-suffering! –
motionlessly
and clearly – endlessly! –
and as if the morning was unwavering
in me: as in the world: absolutely:

and there they placed that place
in the midst of others related
to them:

place I once knew! –

it shone
like an hour of happiness:

with a high
clear centre:

hawthorn – keeping silent beside the singing
like god keeping silent – behind the resounding Word:

keeping silent – with a personality untouched:

one touch – and that is: *no more God*

2

AND: LIKE A WHITE LEAF

in the dust nothing conspicuous . . . only death resounds:

to god – a cry?
he – on the surface of the dust:

what then – *chink of light?*
o not the treasure of a victim:

not an exhibition! . . . not sounds and psalms:

but *dazzle and accept*:

and *be open* – how much *there is* that comes to light:

o *jesus – silence!* . . .

111

ONCE MORE: IN THE INTERMISSIONS OF DREAM

      what is looking
      is always discontinuous:

      and the day! and the world! . . .

      the unique is
      the unintermittent –

      it has features
      the soul glides over:

      like dust! –

      and the light of the looker
      is never unveiled! –

      and the shifting dust:

      unshone-on! –

      crumbles away

FROM THE RUSSIAN OF YEVGENY YEVTUSHENKO

STALIN'S HEIRS

Voiceless that marble.
    Voicelessly the glass flashed.
Voiceless the sentry stood
    in the wind like a man of bronze.
But a ghost of smoke left the coffin.
    A breath squeezed through the cracks
when they carried it out by the Mausoleum doors.
Slowly the coffin hovered,
    its edges grazed the bayonets.
It too was voiceless –
    it too! –
        but voicelessly loud with dread:
inside, a man was
    blackly clenching his embalmed fists,

pressing himself to the cracks,
    pretending to be dead.
He wanted to be able to remember them all,
    all his burial party:
young lads from Ryazan and Kursk,
    rustic recruits:
in order that some day, somehow
    he would gather strength for a sortie
and rise out of the earth
    and fall on them, the rustic dolts.
He's thought up something.
    He's only refreshing himself with a nap.
And I make this appeal now
    to our government, I make this prayer:
to double
    and treble
        the guard at Stalin's slab,
that Stalin may never rise,
    or the past rise with him there.
When I say "past" do you think I mean
    what is most heroic or treasured,
Turksib,
    Magnitka,
        the flag over Berlin?
No, my meaning is
    of a different past, measured
by denunciations,
    by arrests of the innocent,
        by neglect of the good of men.
We sowed seed honestly.
We honestly made metal pour
and honestly marched and
    stood in ranks and were soldierly.
Yet he was afraid of us.
    He believed in a great end but ignored
that the means
    must be worthy
        of the majesty of the goal.
He was frightened.
    Schooled in the laws of the struggle,
he littered the globe with the heirs of his throne.
It looks to me
    as if the coffin has a telephone:
the Enver Hoxhas
    still receive Stalin's instructions.
Has far does the cable from this coffin stretch even yet?

No: Stalin hasn't given in. There are ways
    of dealing with death, he reckons.
Out of the Mausoleum surely it was
    him
        we fetched?
But how are we to fetch
    the Stalin out of Stalin's successors?
Some of his heirs trim roses in retirement,
yet secretly trust
    such retirement is temporary.
Some too
    are first at the microphone abusing Stalin but
these are the ones
    who when night comes
        yearn after the old story.
You can see how today
    it's hardly by chance that the heirs
of Stalin go down with thromboses.
    To them, who were once his props,
the days when the labour camps
    are empty are disasters,
the times when halls overflow
    for the reading of poetry are a blot.
The Party has told me
    I shall not cease
        from mental fight.
If someone repeats, "The fight
    is over!" – I have no skill
        to bury my disquiet.
So long as Stalin's heirs go
    walking in the light,
I'll feel him,
    Stalin, in the Mausoleum yet.

Alexander Scott

FROM THE ANONYMOUS ANGLO-SAXON

SEAMAN'S SANG

Anent mysel I'll tell ye truly:
hou, stravaigan the sea in trauchlesome days,
aye tholan the dunts o time,
I've borne strang stounds in my breist,
kennan my ship the hame o monie cares.
Amang the coorse girn o the swaws I've taen my pairt,
keepan the nichtwatch close i the ship's bows
whan she drave alangside craigs. Nippit wi cauld
my feet were lucken in frost
by chynes o ice, tho wae was greetan then
het roun my hert, and hunger scartit to threids
my sea-forfochten saul. Och, thon's what he daesna ken,
him that bides happy at hame,
hou I, wearied and waesome, amang the icecauld sea,
traivelled throu the winter far awa,
far frae my kinsfowk,
and hung about wi ice and hard hail's onding,
naething to hear but the scraich o the sea,
the icy faem, and whiles the caa o the swan,
and aa the glee I got was the gannet's sang,
the soun o the seal instead o menfowk's lauchter,
the sea-maw's maen instead o the drinkin o drams.
Storms gaed duntan the stanie scaurs, and back the tirricks sung
wi icy feathers, and aye the eagle scraiched,
droukit in faem. Then nane o my kinsfowk
micht lowse the sairness frae my hert.
Little he kens, that ains life's guidliness,
bydan at hame wi scantlin o hardship,
and purpie-proud frae the booze, hou aften wearied
yet I maun byde on the breist o the sea.
The nicht cam doun wi snaw frae the north,
the warld was chyned by ice, and hail was faain,
cauldest o corn. Yet nou gae tyauvan thegither
the thochts o my hert, on the muckle watters
to set mysel agin the stramash o the sea.
Heat in my hert forever forces
my saul to traivel far frae hame
and find the lands o fremmit fowk.
There's nane sae heich o hert i the warld,
sae guid at the giein o gifts, sae swack in 's youth,
in deeds sae dauntie, the laird's delyte,

but aye he yearns to stravaig the sea,
dreean whatever the weird o the fates micht be.
He has nae hert for the clarsach, nor for the winnin o gowd,
nor joy o a wife, nor joy o the warld,
nor in aucht forbye the jowan swaws,
for aye a yearnin yarks him awa til the sea.
Branches tak flouer, the burghs graw bonnie,
the parks look braw, the warld newbricht again,
and aathing steers the gleg young hert
to traivel (him that hauds sic thochts)
far awa ayont the howes o the sea.
The gowk is makkan his greetan maen,
simmer's herald sings and bodes o dule,
coorse wi care for the hert. Aye, thon's what they dinna ken,
them wi the siller, what some maun thole
whas traivel taks them furdest weys awa.
But nou my thochts hing owre my hert,
my saul wi the sea
gaes far owre the hame o the whales
til the ends o the earth, comes back til me
hungert and yearnan, the lane stravaiger scraichs
and forces my hert to fare til the faem
ower the streitch o the sea.

William Neill

FROM THE ITALIAN OF GUIDO CAVALCANTI

SONNETS

1

Ochon, ma leddie did ye nivir see
yon yin wha pit his haund atour ma hairt
whan I spak quaitlie, saftlie? I wes feart
o thon sair dunts he micht hae dune tae me,
for he wes Luve made oor discoverie,
an ercher, swippert cam frae Syrian airt
wha cairries at his belt a deidlie dairt,
an here he bides, sae fowk maun shairlie dee.

Siccan a lowe he brocht oot frae yir een,
sae strang the flain ma breist wes stoundit sair
an frae yir companie I fled awa;
but fell Daith kythed tae meet me rinnan thair
an brocht alang his muckle stangs an teen
that gar us grane, an the sair tears tae faa.

2

Athin ye hae the flouers an the green
an awthing skyre an lusum tae the sicht;
lik the suin's sel yir bonnie face is bricht,
tint is his warth sic bewtie hesna seen.
Nae ither in this warld hes ever been
sae bonnie or sae fu o lusum licht:
siccar is he again wha fears luve's micht
an bi sic lusumness is made luve's frien.

An aw the weemin in yir companie,
bi yir ain luve are they made lusum tae:
sae nou I ask thaim o thair courtasie
wha best is able, lat hir honour dae
an dearlie haud yir rule in majestie,
syne bi yir bewtie, that ye shairlie hae.

117

Antonia Stott

FROM THE ITALIAN OF SALVATORE QUASIMODO

LAMENT FOR THE SOUTH

The red moon, the wind, your colouring
of woman of the North, the snow . . .
My heart is on these grasslands now,
in these waters shadowed by the mists.
I have forgotten the sea, the deep
conch blown by the Sicilian shepherds,
the sing-song of the carts along the roads
where the carob-tree trembles in the smoke of stubble-fields,
I have forgotten the passing of herons and cranes
in the air of the green plateaux
for the lands and rivers of Lombardy.
But a man cries everywhere the fate of his country.
No one will ever take me back to the South.

Oh, the South is tired of dragging its dead
down to the banks of malarial swamps,
is tired of solitude, tired of chains,
it is tired of the curses
in its mouth of all the races
that have shouted death with the echoes of its wells,
that have drunk the blood of its heart.
For this its children go back to the mountains,
lay their horses under a cover of stars,
eat acacia flowers by the ambush posts
newly red, again red, again red.
No one will ever take me back to the South.

And so this evening laden with winter
is still ours, and here I repeat to you
my absurd counterpoint
of tenderness and anger,
a lament of love without love.

FROM THE ITALIAN OF EDOARDO SANGUINETI

1

EROTOPÆGINA

III

Grab this mercury, this cold gum, this honey, this sphere
of arid glass; carefully measure the head of our
child, don't twist now his imperceptible
foot:
    into your nipple it's now time you turned
a prolonged continent of lamps, the obsessive breath of critical
gardens, the lazy whales of the belly, nettles
and wine, nausea and rust;
                  for every road will soon want
to rush to him, an umbilical hernia carve
its smoky profile, some hippopotamus present him
with its teeth of dandruff and black phosphorus:
                        avoid the wind,
crowded places, jugglers, insects;
and at six months he will be able to double his own weight, see the goose,
clasp the dressing-gown, watch the falling bodies;
tear him therefore from his life of seaweeds and globules, of small knots,
and uncertain lobes:
             his wail will conquer your liquid wounds
and his oblique butter eyes will correct these centuries without name!

IV

inside you he was asleep like a dry fibroma, like a thin tape-
                    worm, like a dream;
now he treads on the gravel, now shakes his own shadow; now he
                    shrieks,
swallows, urinates, having for ever awaited the taste
of camomile, the temperature of the hare, the noise
              of hail,
the shape of the roof, the colour of straw:
              inexorably time
has turned towards his days; the earth is offering confused
              images;
will he recognise the goat, the peasant, the cannon?
not for these scissors was he really longing, not for this pear,
when he trembled in your sac of opaque membranes.

119

2

PURGATORY OF HELL

XV

beyond that purgatory of gardens (and the white light, and the iron
chairs); and (also) beyond the birds dying
on the green branches:
                              there is the Galerie Vivienne;
beyond us, then, there exists that true cemetery (as I said): three long
boxes of picture-postcards, all written, and stamped:
                                             all to be read.

3

LA DOLCE VITA

II

this is not nostalgia: this is death —
                      this dead fish-pond of sleepy eels,
raving (and hypnotically hysterical) eels:
                      oh grieved wonder, how
unrestrainedly you conquer the blood, you consume! thin ancient images
how exhausted is the pitiless game! hypocrisy is the wavering regret:
a world cannot die: the phantoms live
                              and what is cruel here
is only this education of the feelings and, to funeral candelabra,
the vain error of the winds, the fairytale-corpse of the erotic minstrel, life.

George Kay

FROM THE ITALIAN OF EUGENIO MONTALE

1

BAGNI DI LUCCA

Between the thud of chestnuts
and the moaning of the stream
which join their sounds as one
the heart holds back.

Winter too quickly ripening when the north wind
strikes shivers. I come forward
upon the bank which releases the white
of day in ice.

Marble, branching –
                              and at a shaking down
leaves propellering, arrowed,
into the ditch.

The last flock is passing in the mist
of its breathing.

2

YOU KNOW IT

You know it: I have to lose you again and I cannot.
Like a well-aimed shot every work disturbs,
every cry and even the salty breath
that overflows
from the quays and makes the unlit spring
of Sottoripa.

Region of iron and masts
in one forest in the dust of nightfall.
A long buzzing comes from out there,
harrows like nails upon glass. I look for the sign
lost now, the only pledge I had, freely granted,
from you.
                  And hell is certain.

3

UNDER THE RAIN

A murmur; and your house is blurred
as in the haze of remembering –
and the palm runs teardrops now that, grim,
the dissolution weighs that keeps confined
in the sultry hothouse even the naked
hopes and the thought which gnaws.

"Por amor de la fiebre" . . . one whirling
takes me along with you. Flaring red,
an awning there, a window is shut.
On the motherly slope is walking now,
egg-shell that goes into the oozing slime,
small life in the flutter of shade and light.

Your record wheezed *Adiós muchachos, compañeros
de mi vida*, from the courtyard:
and the masquerade is dear to me if still
beyond the milling-round of chance
the leap is there that carries me back
to your path.

I follow the bright dashes and far away,
in cloud-line, the smoke trailed by a ship.
A rift is traced out . . .
                         For you I realize
what the stork braves when lifting up
his flight from the misty pinnacle
he strokes on his way towards the Cape.

4

CORRESPONDENCES

Now that in the distance a mirage
of vapours wavers and breaks, to scatter,
a new thing is announced, among the trees, by the peal
of the green woodpecker.

The hand which stretches to the underwood
and pierces through the web
of the heart with littered points,
is the one that ripens nightmares of gold
at the mirror of ponds
when the car, rumbling loud,
of Bacchus returns, bringing wild yelps
of rams from burnt patches in the hills.

Are you too coming back, flockless shepherdess,
to sit upon my stone?
I recognize you; but I cannot guess
what you read beyond flights that wander on
the pass. I vainly ask the plain where dreams
a moment's haze between shots and flashes
on scattered roofs – I ask the expresses'
hid fever on the coast that steams.

5

THE SHADOW OF THE MAGNOLIA

The shadow of the Japanese magnolia
lies less thickly now that the purple-tinged buds
have fallen. In bursts a cicada thrums
from on high. It is no longer
the time of voices in unison,
Clizia, time of the boundless god
who devours his faithful, granting them new blood.
Giving all was easier, dying
at the first flutter, the first encounter
with the enemy, a game. Now there begins
the harder way: but not you wasted
by sun and rooted, and no less tender
fieldfare who pass above the cold
wharf-sides of your river – not you delicate
fugitive in whom zenith nadir cancer
capricorn stayed undefined
so that the war might be in you and in him adoring
on you the wounds of your Bridegroom, you are not
bent by the shiver of frost . . . The others fall back
and crumple. The file that minutely
cuts will go silent, the empty casing

of the one who sang will soon be powder
of glass underfoot, the shadow is livid –
it is the autumn, is the winter, it is the beyond
which leads you and into which I throw myself, mullet
leapt clear of water in the new moon.

                                                    Goodbye.

6

THE EEL

The eel, the siren
of cold seas who leaves the Baltic
journeying to reach our seas,
our estuaries, our rivers
which it mounts deep down, under the opposing
spate, from branch to branch and then
from hairline to hairline, narrowing
more and more inward, more into the heart
of the flint stone, slithering
between runnels of slime until one day
a light fired down from chestnut trees
glitters its streak in unmoving pools
in the stream-beds which fall away
from Apennine cliffs to the Romagna;
the eel, torch, whiplash,
arrow of love on earth
which only our gullies or the dried-up
Pyrennean streams lead back
to a paradise that fecundates;
the green soul questing
life where nothing but
blazing heat and desolation gnaw,
the spark that is saying
everything begins when everything seems
to char black, a buried stump;
short-lived iris, the rainbow, twin-sister
of the one your forehead sets
and you let shine entire among the sons
of men plunged in your mud, can you
not take her for a sister?

ANCIENT ONE

Ancient one, I am drunken with the voice
that escapes from your mouths when they lift up
like green bells and heave upon each other
heave backwards and then go free.
the home of my far-away summers
was by your side, as you know,
there in the country where the sun broils
and mosquitoes cloud upon the air.
Today, once more, I am overcome
my sea, by your presence, but no longer
think myself worthy of the grave warning tone
that comes in your breath. You told me first of all
that the tiny seething
of my heart was simply an impulse
of yours; that in my depth of being there was
your perilous law: to be vast, manifold,
and yet, to be bound:
and so to clear myself of every filthiness
as you do who dash upon the shores
among driftwood, seaweed, starfishes,
the fruitless rubbish of your void.

Alastair Mackie

FROM THE ITALIAN OF GIACOMO LEOPARDI

TO SILVIA

Silvia, d'ye still mind
yon time o your mortal life
when fairheid leamed
in the lauchin sklents o your een
and gled and pensefou ye stood syne
at the doorsill o maidenhood?

The quait chaumers
and the closes ootby
thrummed wi your perpetual sang
as ye sat thrang at your hoose work
canty tee at the gowden future
ye ettled to hae.
It was the scented May, and this gait
gaed your day.

Whiles I wid quit my pleasant book-lear
and my thumb-tashed blads
faur youth and my sel's best pairt
was spent, and fae the balconies
o my father's house I'd listen
for your voice liltin
and the birr o your eident hand
caain the tyaavin loom.
I'd look at the lown lyft,
the gowden wynds, the fruit gairdens,
on ae side the far sea, the hill on the tither.
O nae man's tongue can tell
whit I felt inside mysel!

O whit sweet thochts, whit braw hopes,
whit lowpins o the hert, Silvia, my lass!
Bonny the face that human life itsel,
and fate had for us baith.
When I mind o sic gowden promises
A wersh sensation
weighs on me, doon-moued,
and I turn to murn
my black ill-chance.

O nature, nature whit wey
d'ye nae gie us back
aa that ye promised aince?
Whit wey this cheatrie
against the sons o men?

Afore the winter wizzent aa the grass
ye wede awa, sweet lass,
An onfall focht wi you and won.
Ye didna see the flourish o your years.
Naething nou could melt your hert
wi sweet praises, now o your hair's black locks,
now o the blate love-looks o your een,
nor did your girl-friens
forgaither on holidays
to crack wi you anent love.

In a wee my hopes deid ana.
I was weirded tee,
my years had nae youtheid.
O how ye passed, how ye passed awa
my frien, begrutten hope,
dear companion o my early years!
Is this yon same world? And sic-like
its delichts, its works, its ootcomes
we twa conversed aboot atween oorsels?
Is this the weird o human kind?
Ye drappit doun, poor lass,
afore the ootcome o the truth,
and fae hyna awa ye pintit wi your hand
to clay-cauld death and an unkent tomb.

THE QUAIT AIFTER THE TEMPEST

The onding's blawn owre.
I hear the birds' sangschaw, and the hen
struttin back to the street,
keckles aince mair. Look nou,
a blue bore braks yonder in the west
abeen the hill-taps.
The country side begins to fair up
and clear in the howe the river leams.

Herts kittle up again, in ilkie airt
the steer and din o labour
turns to its daily-darg.
The workman wi his tools in hand
braks into sang, een stelled on the droukit lyft
ootby his door. A wummin body rins oot
ram-stam fae her hoose
ettlin aifter the prize
o bein first to fill her cog
wi the caller rain watter.
And the herb-troker traiks fae close to close,
aince mair his daily cry rings oot
"Wha'll buy? Wha'll buy?"
Ah, there's the sun's face keekin oot
and smilin doun on hill and toun.
Servin lassies throw open the winnocks,
balconies and chaumers.
I hear fae the high-gate
the hyne awa ting-tang o horses' harness bells,
the craikin cairt o the traiveller
as he taks the gate for hame.

Every hert is blithesome.
Was ever life, as now,
so douce and lichtsome
when man turns to
his day-darg afresh
wi so muckle passion?
Or undertaks new ploys?
When is he less fashed
by mindin o his trauchles?
Pleisure's the bairn o dool,
joy is toom, it is the fruit
o terror lang past.
The man that has loathed life
chitters wi fear at death.
Hence in this lang torment
clay-cauld, mum, white-faced
men shiver and sweat when
they see in the lyft
forgaither to their hairm,
levin-flaucht, clood and wind.

O glad-handit Nature
are these syne your gifts?
Is this the happiness you offer
to mortal man? The road oot
o anguish is blessin enough
and tears ye sow wi a braid hand.
Dool springs full-born fae itsel.
The pleisure that's born oot
o some ill, by some miracle
stands to your gain. O world o men
dear to the eternal gods,
happy enough were ye gien
the respite to draw ae breath, jist,
aifter each hert-scaud,
mair blessed still gin aa these ills
are cured by death itsel.

FROM THE RUSSIAN OF FYODOR TYUTCHEV

INSOMNIA

1

The dreary jowin o the clock
the nicht-time dreich and wan,
it's the ootlin tongue o the universe,
the clear conscience o each man.

Wha hears it withoot a grue
mid the calm souch o the cosmos,
yon muffled keenin o the 'oors
wi their spaeman's fareweel voice?

I doot the world's an orphan,
it's the doom-'oor, we're owretane,
in the great war o nature
we're left wi oorsels alane.

Afore us oor haill life stands
like a wraith at the earth's rim,
oor times, oor friens, whiten wi't
in the hyne awa mirkenin.

While the new green generations
hae sprootit up in the sun,
oor age, oor times and us langsyne
are copt to oblivion.

Only whiles in the mid o the nicht
when its doosome rites are dane
yon deid-bell gab o metal
murns for us nou and then.

2

KYTHINGS

There's ae 'oor o the nicht
when the universe faas deid-lown
yon's the time that unco sichts
and ferlies kyth abune,
and thro the husht kirk o the lyft
earth's chariot rowes roun.

Like Chaos owre the watter's face
the pit-mirk thickens syne,
the yirth like the haud o Atlas
is grippt in oblivion.
Only the gods sair vex the Muses' eyes,
her sleep ghaist-rid wi eerie fantasies.

3

At the ootset o the back-end comes
a sharp snap when the season's spell-bound:
days are lee-lang crystals
and the gloamins leam.

Whaur aince the soople suckle dandert
and the corn-ears souched, toom space fills
the landscape syne. Nou on an idle fur
the spinnly threid o a moose-eab winks.

The air is teemed oot, bird pleep faas lown,
winter's snell gusts are still hyne aff,
and nou het azure skails its caller spaes
onto the hairst field's lowsin time.

FROM THE FRENCH OF ARTHUR RIMBAUD

THE DRUCKEN BOAT

I felt nae mair the haalyers airtin me
as I gaed doun the abeigh watter floods,
Reidskins had nailed them tae their pentit poles
and ta'en for their skirlin' shootin'-brods.

I didna care a doit for the haill crew,
I cairriet Fleemish corn or English claith,
the rivers let me be tae float at wull,
the haalyers' stishie endit wi' their daith.

Me, I flew last winter dafter nor a bairn
intill the gousterous tide-rips o' the sea.
The peninsulas wi' their halsers lowsed
och, the hullaballoo they had tae drie!

The tempest sained my mid-sea waukenins,
I dansit lichter nor a cork upo' the faem
fowk ca' the eternal showdin' o' the drooned,
and niver missed the lantrins' glaikit een.

Green watter, drookin' a' my cockle-boat,
was sweeter nor soor aipples til a bairn,
it sweeled awa the wine-stains and the boke
and skailed my rudder and my graipple-airn.

Sinsyne I've drookit i' the poem o' the sea,
wi' its maskin o' starns, its white spilth o' milk,
I gobbled greens and blues; and in a dwam whiles,
a drooned corp draps doun, a blae and spell-boond hulk.

Raveries o' the brack, the slaw rhythms
dye the azures neth the daylicht's iron eer,
and stranger nor booze, vaster nor oor leids
love's reid and sauty bree is barmin' here.

I ken the lifts the levin fire has rived,
tides, currents, undersooks; the nichts, I ken,
the day-daw upskailin' like a crood o' doos,
and whiles I've seen whit man has thocht he's seen.

I've seen sic horrors tashin' the laich sun
and leam on the blue gealin' latitudes,
the swaws, Greek actors on an antique stage,
row hyne awa the cauld grue o' their moods.

Nichts I dreamt o', green wi the bleeze o' snaw,
kisses slaw spielin' till the ocean's broo,
the ebbin' and flawin' o' unkent sap,
the sea-fire singin' in yalla and blue.

I followed haill months, the ramstam bullheids
o' the swaal, as they bugled on the skairs,
and niver thocht their gruntles wad be branked
and wind-broken, on the Marys' eenbricht spurs.

Faith, my bows hae duntit unco Floridas
o' flooers wi' human skin and panther een,
watergaws airched like bridles neth the seas'
horizons, beast shoals o' a pale sea-green.

I've seen the hotter o' enormous quags,
a Leviathan was foostin' in their nets,
jaws o' watter in a deid-lown sea
and far airts coupin into watterpits.

Glaciers, siller suns, nacreous swaws, aizle lifts,
grim wrack-ships i' the boddom o' broon gulfs,
whaur muckle serpents etten up wi' mawks
drap, like knurly trees, the black reek o' their guffs.

I ettled to show the bairns yon doradoes,
the gowd and singin' fishes o' the sea,
faem-flooers lulled me, win'-bufft frae the roads,
and unkent blufferts gaed me wings tae flee.

Whiles a martyr, forfairn wi' poles and zones.
O sweet the rowin' o' the sabbin' seas,
their ghaist-flooers' yalla sookers raise tae me
and I bade, like a wummin on her knees . . .

My peninsula bobbit wi' the skraich
o' blond-eed birds, their shite and their fracaw,
I scuddit on, athort my bruckle lines
the drooned gaed arselins doon tae sleep awa . . .

A tint boat, fankled i' the hair o' wicks
the skail-win' skited me tae birdless blue,
the Airn-cleds and navies o' the Hanse
wad ne'er hae fished my carcass up, blin-fou.

My pipe luntin', my crew the purply haars
I howkit up the firmament's reid wa'
frauchtit wi' braw galshochs for the makars,
azure snotters and solar hazel-raw.

Black sea horses allemanded me
sailin' my spale-boord neth electric moons,
July, timmerin' the sea-blue elements
let fa' the birstlin' funnels o' monsoons.

I shook tae hear, a hunner mile awa
the rut o' Behemoths, the Maelstroms' manes,
eternal star-glint o' immobile blue,
I miss ye, Europe, and your auld parpanes.

I've seen the archipelagoes o' starns
deleerit lifts open tae the voyager,
– is't in yon boddomless nichts ye ligg asleep
o million gowden birds, o future Virr? –

I've grat ower muckle. The hertbrak o' the dawns!
Baith sun and moon are a hertscauld tae me,
a soor love swalled me wi' its dozent drams.
O let my keel brak! O let me gang tae sea!

A' I'd want o' Europe is a gutter
cauld and dreich, whaur aboot the set o' day
a wee loon on his hunkers sails a boat
as bruckle as a butter-flee in May.

Steeped in your langour, swaws, I canna cut
athort the wake o' traders, I'm deid deen,
or conter the prood pennants o' the fleets
or row aneth the prison-hulks' gash een.

FROM THE RUSSIAN OF ANNA AKHMATOVA

1

JULY 1914

I

There's a smell o burnin. The dry peat
was alunt fower weeks in the bogs.
The-day the birds nae langer pleep
na mair the aspen shogs.

The sun's a sign o the wrath o the Lord
since Pace nae rain has wat the grun
An ae-leggit man cam by the yaird
and said there aa his lane.

"Dreidfu days are drawin near
the yird shall be croodit wi fresh lairs,
hunger and pest and erd-din fear
and the eclipse o aa the stars.

The foe shall never rive abreid
oor mitherland to dae his will.
God's mither her white shawl shall spreid
abune us and oor muckle dool."

II

Oot frae the burnin wids there eems
the juniper's bonny smell.
Sodgers' wives murn owre their weans
widdas gar the clachan wail.

Nae in vain the offert prayers,
the yirth was langin for the weet.
Skinkled owre the howkt up furs
a skiftin reid and het.

The toom lyft was laich, sae laich,
and saft the voice that prays,
"To your haly days they dae skaith
and cast lots for your claes."

2

I mind o ye but little ava
and I'm no that tane wi your fate;
but slicht tho the tryst was 'tween us twa
my soul tholes the stoond o't yet.

I ettle to pass your reid hoose by
abeen the glaury watter-side
but I ken as I pass your reid hoose by
I sair vex your sun-droukt quiet.

Tho it wisna you that owre my lips
boued doun for my love fu fain
tho it wisna you in gowden leids
immortalised my pain

Still, I glammer the future
when the nichts are midnicht blue
and I foreken for certain sure
anither tryst wi you.

3

In the gairden the music's voice
dirls wi a dool untellable.
O keen and caller is the smell
o oysters in a dish o ice.

He said "I'm a leal-hertit frien"
and wi that he toucht my dress.
O it wisna like ony embrace
the touch yon hands hae gien.

Ye'd look at jimp rouch-riders,
straik a cat or a bird like yon,
There was nocht but lauchter in 's een
'neth the licht gowd o his breears.

Aneth the drifts o reek the tune
the sabbin violins sing, "Praise nou
to heaven ye're aa your lane
for the first time him ye loo."

FROM THE RUSSIAN OF OSIP MANDELSTAM

1

INSOMNIA

Sleeplessness. Homer. Sails furthstreekit.
I've read half-weys doun the lang leet o ships;
yon clunkin cleckin, yon crane-like skein
that upskailed owre Hellas aince, lang syne.

Whaur do ye sail till like a wedge o cranes
oarin for ootlin airts? (The gods' faem braks
on the heids o kings.) O Greek warriors
whit's Troy to you, gin Helen werena there?

The sea and Homer baith – love means aathing.
Wha will I listen till? And nou Homer hauds his wisht.
And the haroosh and splairge o the Black sea's rhetoric
cairries its wechtit thunder to my bedded heid.

2

LENINGRAD

Back to my hame-toun, as kenspeckle as tears,
as my veins, as a bairn's dose o the mumps.
Back hame . . . so cowp doun quick a moufae
o the cod-liver ile o the riverside lamplichts.
Quick nou, and mak oot the short December day
whaur the eerie tar is seepit in egg-yoke.
Ach, Petersburg, I've nae mind to dee jist yet.
Petersburg, I still hae addresses to hand,
they speak to me in deid men's tongues.
I live on the dark stair-heid, the doorbell's skirl
howks slivers o skin fae my brou.
The lee-lang nicht I wait for my welcome guests
ruggin at the chained sneck o the door.

3

STRAVAIGER

I feel the grue o untholeable terror
in the company o uncanny heichts,
I' fain for the swalla steekin the air
I love the bell-tooer's brak-neck flichts.

And I micht be the auld-world danderer
abeen the cleuchs o air on shoogly boords
I hear the snaw-ba's gaitherin thunder growe
and eternity ding oot in steeny 'oors.

Let it be syne! But I'm nae yon stravaiger
gane in a skinkle o cassent greenery.
The truth is – dowieness sings inside me.
O aye, there is an avalanche in the hills!
And my haill soul's in the ting-tang o the bells,
but music winna spare me infinity's black gowls.

FROM THE ITALIAN OF SALVATORE QUASIMODO

1

ON THE SAUCH BOUGHS

And whit wey could we mak poems
wi the fremmit jackboot on oor hert,
amang the leavins o the deid i the squares,
on the gress dour wi ice,
to the lamb-baein o the bairns,
the black skelloch o the mither meetin her son
crucifeet on the telegraph pole?
On the sauch boughs for an offrin
oor lyres were hung forby
sweein licht in the waesome wind.

2

SCRIEVE

This deid-dour silence in the streets,
this dwaumy wind that slips noo
laich through the deid leaves or lifts again
to the colours o the fremmit flags . . .
mebbe the sair need to say jist ae word
afore the lyft aince mair mirkens
ower anither day, mebbe sweerness,
oor meanest fau . . . This
isna life, this fearsome dark dirlin
o the hert, this peety,
it's nocht but a game the blood plays
when death's in flooer. O my douce gazelle
I mind that geranium o yours
bleezin on the bullet-howkit wa!
Och, does death nae mair console the livin,
nae even the death through love?

3

Day aifter day; damnèd words and the blood
and gowd. I ken ye, my peers, monsters o the yirth.
Poetry has gaen doun afore your bite,
and the douce cross has left us.
Nae mair can I win back to my Elysium.
We'll bigg tombs on the sea strand, the huggert fields,
but nae monuments shall mark the heroes.
Mony's the time death has joukit us;
the air soughed wi a monotonous reeshle o leaves
like the watter-craw in the heather
that mounts a clood when the sirocco blaws.

Burns Singer

FROM THE POLISH OF JOZEF CZECHOWICZ
(with Jerzy Peterkiewiez)

GRIEF

M Y hair is greying but it slants with light
when strands of wind lift it, a chandelier,
that I must always carry through these hollow streets.
The swallows twitter by the river and
it's not so heavy – just my head.
Walk. Walk on.

Walk. Walk. And watch: the scenes, the dreams, the feasts:
cracked glass adorns the synagogues with scars;
a flame gulps up the coarse thick hawser;
the flame of love
denudes us.

The nations are most greedy when they roar.
They cannot whimper like a hungry man.

This evening heavily upon the world
spreads its low length as nostrils scent
red milk from bared volcanoes.
Deciphering which stranger: Who are you?
and multiplying magically through
our own torn selves, I shoot my names, and die.
I die, who huddled with my plough in furrows;
I, a brisk lawyer, drown in instructions;
I, in chlorine, I choking, I dying, gas!
and I am the girl who sleeps with the primrose;
and I, a child, in a live torch, live;
and I at my market stall with the blaze of a bomb;
and I am the madman who's hanged for the fire:
I am my signature, my mother's illiterate cross.

But now the harvest
glows with deep noise.

And how can the river untorture itself and unrust
our brotherly blood before, among us,
the colonnades rise, the mathematical eagles?
A blizzard of swallows will come
with a whirl that swirls my head,
but through the darkness that the birds give wing
I shall walk, I shall walk on.

139

Alistair Fowler

FROM THE ITALIAN OF GIACOMO LEOPARDI

1

THE INFINITE

They were always friends, this hill where no one comes
And this hedge here, that from so large a part
Of the ultimate horizon shuts out the eye.
Sitting in contemplation, I form unbounded
Distances on the other side, silences
Past man, and deepest calm. Then my heart comes
Close to taking fright; and, as the breeze
Rustles among the leaves, I keep comparing
That infinite silence to this small voice: recall
Eternity, and the seasons that are gone,
And the living present one, the sound of it.
And so my thought founders, lost in this
Immensity; and it seems to me a gentle thing
To suffer shipwreck in this pacific ocean.

2

CHORUS OF THE DEAD

Only enduring thing in the world: to you
At last every creature turns;
In you, death, rests,
Our undefended being –
Not happy, but secure
From the anguish of former times. Endless night
Darkens laborious thought
In the uncertain mind;
The dried-up spirit feels its drive to hope,
To desire, quite give out:
So it is freed from trouble and anxiousness,
And wears out vacant slow
Ages unwearied. We
Lived; and as the troubled recollection
Of fearful wraith and sweating dream flits
Around an infant's mind,
So the memory of life
Remains with us; but far,
Our remembering, from fear. What
Were we? and what that phase –
Grievous, childish – that bore the name of life?

Today life seems to us
A mysterious, marvellous thing,
Just as unknown death
To the thought of those alive. As, when we lived,
Our naked being shrank from death, so
Now it recoils from the vital flame,
Not happy, but secure;
Since fate denies the state
Of being happy to mortals and to the dead.

3

VILLAGE SATURDAY

Towards the decline of day
The lass comes back from the fields
With her truss of hay, and brings
A posy in her hand, of violets and roses:
Her usual holiday system,
To make her blouse and hair pretty tomorrow.
On the step, the old wife sits
With neighbours and spins, facing over to where
Day is lost at last;
And rambles on, renewing the good old times,
When she'd wear her holiday best
– Still slender, then, and spry –
And would dance the night away with the men she had
As partners of her fairer time.

Already all the air
Duskens, the cloudy sky
Grows pale again, again the shadows fall
From hills and roofs in the young moon's blanching light.
Now the clang of bells
Gives promise of holiday to come;
And at the sound you'd say
That you took heart again.

Armies of children shout
In the little square, leap
This way and that, make a happy noise;
The farm hand meanwhile returns
Whistling to a bite of supper, and ruminates
On his day of rest. Then
When every other light around is out
And all else quiet,

You hear the joiner, the patter of his hammer, his saw's
Sigh, as he works away
By lantern light in his shuttered shop; strains,
Hurries to have the piece
Finished before the dawn's critical light.

This is the welcomest day of all the seven,
Full of hope and joy:
Tomorrow the slow hours
Will bring tedium, sadness;
All will go back in thought to their usual work.

Mischievous little rascal:
This blossom time of your life
Is like a day that's full of merrymaking,
A clear, cloudless day
Before your holiday-life.
Enjoy it, lad: this is a pleasant way
To be, a happy time.
I won't say more; but may it not be too
Grim, that your holiday to come is slow to come.

Derek Bowman

FROM THE GERMAN OF JOHANN WOLFGANG VON GOETHE

TALISMAN

Both sides of breathing are a blessing,
The drawing in air, likewise its releasing.
The former oppresses, the latter refreshes;
So wonderfully existence meshes.
See you praise God when He presses you,
And thank Him when He lets you go.

FROM THE GERMAN OF HANS MAGNUS ENZENSBERGER

PASSAGE FOR AN UPPER-SCHOOL READER

read no odes, my son, read the railway-guides:
they're more exact. roll up the charts,
before it gets too late. be on your guard, don't sing.
the day is coming when they'll once again be posting
notices on gates and sticking signs on people who
won't play. learn to pass incognito, learn more than me:
to change your quarters, passport, face.
get to know all about petty treachery,
the routine dirty let-out. the encyclicals
are good for lighting fires;
the manifestoes – for wrapping salt and butter
for the defenceless. anger and patience are required
to blow into the lungs of power
the fine and deadly dust, ground
by those who know the score,
who've learnt what's what, from you.

FROM THE GERMAN OF GUNTHER KUNERT

1

POEM ON POEMS

More than a poem
is for instance: no poem,
for the non-poem lives
as gentle tepidity of inspiration:
sense of environment
of a drop in water.
The body feels safe.
The heart feels nothing.
The scales are balanced.
The plumb hangs still.

Poem is state,
that the poem destroys
by means of
emerging from itself.

2

DECYPHERING SHADOWS

Who would know how to read
the letters which are not:
mossy tile from the roof
charred wood still from the war
blocks of shattered concrete

and the shadows in the morning
corrected by the shadows of evening
in the rows of houses
between which
all truths stand.

3

TWOFOLD MONOLOGUE – SHORT-CIRCUITED

O to our children, the computers,
o their impotent sympathy for us:
with tongues punched to bits they speak
logically and aimlessly, because logic, because aim
applied to fathers, means o only waste:
irrational irrationality
of electron-rapid stationary cubes,
from top to bottom nothing but brain
that thinks and thinks
and thinks:
O to our servants, the oxygenated idiots
and ah
and woe to the lymphatic ghosts
incapable of true logic, of pure aim:
O to our childlike manufacturers: O O O O
O O O O O O O O
OOOOOOOO
oooooo

4

BERLIN AFTERNOON

In summer to an overcast sky
in summer to gentle rain
in summer in the cool of old apartments
between the imaginative capacity of dark wallpapers:
to lie
and listen to the metropolitan railway
the muffled impact on sleepers
trotting of hackney-carriages
staccato of machines worked by hand
in blown-away back closes
perishable play of bodies wafted off
pale in the pallor of intimate beds
hidden behind crumbling stucco
behind the rampant scurvy of old houses
that one sudden afternoon
by bulldozers and cranes contents included

are ungarlanded shifted
from their existence our memory
where their welcomed and lamented transience
comes to rest: in summer
to gentle rain.

5

RAIN

In the world of destroyed images,
of untrustworthy writings
the rain indicates the façades
unequivocally:

Behold my works, damp and
cheerful: spreading
decomposition which is life.
Aqua distillata breeds
nothing: purity
is fearless.

Study the rain: each drop
is true.

George MacBeth

FROM THE FRENCH OF FRANCIS PONGE

From *THE WASP WOMAN*

XIV

First there was the furnace. And then

the half-charred wasp was born, hissing, terrible
    and by no means a matter
of indifference to Men-kind, for they faced

in her burning elegance their abortive
    hunger for speed and for closed
flight through air. And in mine I saw an earthed fire

whose wings gushed out in all directions, and on
    unforeseen trajectories.
It burned as if on offensive missions from

a nest in the ground. Like an engine out of
    control, sometimes it trembled
as though she were not the mistress of her own

destructiveness. So at first that fire spread in
    the earth, crackling, fluttering:
and then when the wings were accomplished, the sexed

wings, the antennaed squadrons broke out on their
    deady business into the
flesh, and their work began to be finished, I

mean, her crime.

XV

In her swarm of words, the abrupt
    waspishness. But wait. Was this
devised flutter in the trench any more than

the weak rebellion of a few seeds, outraged
    by their sower? It was their
own violence that first brought them into his

147

apron. No, go back. This was a fire whose wings
   gushed out in all directions,
and on unforeseen trajectories. And I

faced in her burned elegance my abortive
   hunger for speed and for closed
flight through air. Or must one look further. Here was

the natural world on the wing. Her cruel
   divisions preparing their
offensive against male tyranny. I bared

my forests for their sting. But already her
   banked animosity was
flowing away in random fury. . . .

John Manson

FROM THE FRENCH OF PAUL ÉLUARD

1

OUR LIFE

Our life you made it it is buried
Dawn over a town a fine May morning
On which the earth has closed its fist
Dawn in me seventeen years always brighter
And death comes into me as into a mill

Our life you said so happy to be alive
And to give life to the things we loved
But death has broken the balance of time
Death which comes death which goes death lived through
Death seen eats and drinks at my expense

Dead seen Nusch unseen and harder
Than thirst and hunger to my deserted body
Mask of snow on the earth and under the earth
Spring of tears in the night mask of the blind
My past breaks up I give way to silence

2

SPRING

There are pools on the beach
There are trees in the woods mad with birds
The snow melts on the mountain
The branches of the apple trees shine with so many flowers
That the pale sun fades

It is a winter evening in a very dour world
That I see this spring near you, innocent
There is no night for us
Nothing that dies has a hold on you
And you do not want to be cold

Our spring is a spring which is right

Graham Dunstan Martin

FROM THE FRENCH OF LOUISE LABÉ

SONNETS

1

I live and die; drowning I burn to death,
Seared by the ice and frozen by the fire;
Life is as hard as iron, as soft as breath;
My joy and trouble dance on the same wire.

In the same sudden breath I laugh and weep,
My torment pleasure where my pleasure grieves;
My treasure's lost which I for all time keep,
At once I wither and put out new leaves.

Thus constant Love is my inconstant guide;
And when I am to pain's refinement brought,
Beyond all hope, he grants me a reprieve.

And when I think joy cannot be denied,
And scaled the peak of happiness I sought,
He casts me down into my former grief.

2

While still my eyes have tears to shed, regretting
How joyful time with you has fled away,
While still there's power in my wrist to play,
Your gentleness to gentle music setting,

While still my voice can find the self-command
To sing of you, and overcome a sigh,
While still my soul can other thoughts deny,
And you are all it seeks to comprehend,

I shall not yet desire the embrace of death.
But when I feel the tears dry on my face,
My voice broken, my hand bereft of strength,

My spirit in this mortal dwelling-place
Showing no sign of love, then I shall pray
Death to efface in night my brightest day.

150

1

THE MAGI

Shall we travel as fast as the star?
Hasn't the trip been long enough already?
Shall we succeed in losing at last
that glow between moon and beast,
taking its time?

The snow had embroidered the lands of returning
with its melted flowers where memory is lost.
New companions joined our band,
emerging from the trees like woodcutters.
The Wandering Jew toiled along, his injuries derided.
The black king was wrapped in furs and deadly sick.
The shepherd of hunger is among us,
his blue eyes illuminate his coat of parings
and the furious flock of captive children.

We were going to see joy, so we thought,
the world's joy born in a house hereabouts.
That was at the beginning. Now we don't speak.
We were going to deliver a radiant tomb
marked with a cross by forest torches.

It's a perilous land this, the castles
stealthy behind our backs.
No fires in the inn hearths. The frontiers
shift at dawn under forbidden strokes.
Our palms that broke sandstorms
are weevil-riddled and I fear the night.

Those who waited for us in the wind of the road
have grown tired, chorus their protests.
Through suburbs shuttered at dawn, loveless country,
we pass together and not together
beneath hope's heavy eyelids.
Terror panting like an old nag.

We'll arrive too late, the massacre has begun,
the innocents are lying in the grass.
And we splash up puddles every day in every land.
And the murmur gets hollower, of the dead unrescued
who trusted in our diligence.

The incense has gone rancid in its ivory boxes
and the gold has curdled our hearts like milk.
The girl has given herself to the soldiers,
whom we kept in the ark for her radiance,
the smile on her face.

We are lost. We've been given false directions.
From the very start of the journey.
There was no road, there is no light.
Only a golden cornspike out of a dream,
that the weight of our falling has not swollen.
And we go on, murmuring at ourselves,
on as bad terms as a man
can be with himself.
And the world dreams in our progress
through the grass of the bottom-lands.
And they hope when we have missed our way.

Straying in time's watered silk, the rough meanders
given life by the Child's smile,
knights in quest of the receding birth
of the future that prods us like an ox-herd,
I curse the whole venture, I want to return
to home and plane-tree
to drink the water of my well untroubled by the moon,
and fulfil myself on my terraces, always flat
in the still coolness of my own shadow.

But I cannot be free of this senseless call.

2

EPITAPH

When I present my slate to Nothingness
one day soon,
he won't snigger in my face.
My figures aren't fiddled,
they add up to absolute zero.
Come my son, he'll say with his cold teeth,
to the bosom you deserve.
I shall lie down in his gentleness.

3

SELF-PORTRAIT

Pudgy and mournful,
an opaque pearl bulging his eye,
speech thickened by venison,
bushy as a cross-eyed star,
cracked as a calf running in the moonlight,
steady as a drum buried not far off,
beating stopping then starting again,
verdant as a mould that eats its wall
then smiles,
irreverent of happiness,
having no enviable place,
with straightforward prickly ways,
gauchely rolling his eyes and his r's,
in his childhood's coal and all others,
slowly negating himself, there stands
a human light-projector.

Duncan Glen

FROM THE GERMAN OF STEFAN GEORGE

RESPONSES: THE MISTAKIN

The apostle lay lamentin nicht and day
streekit on the hill that liftit Christ to Heiven.
"Dae you abandon us to despair?
Has your glory made you blin to earth?
Will I ne'er hear your voice again?
Ne'er kiss your hem and your feet?
Gie me a sign. But nae whisper."
Then cam a fremmit ane: "Brither speak!
Your face burns wi agony.
It will sear me if I dinna sooth it!"
"Your words dae nae guid . . . Let me be!
I look for my Lord. He has forsaken me."
The fraim went. The apostle knelt.
Wi anguished cry . . . for by the licht of Heiven
strang in that place he kent
through blin pain and owre weak hope
he hadnae seen: the Lord had been and gane.

FROM THE GERMAN OF RAINER MARIA RILKE

LAMENT

Aathing faur gone
and lost,
I think, the starn,
a brichtness welcomed in,
extinct for licht years.
I think, in the barge,
that passed,
a voice feart.
In the house a knock
went died . . .
In which house?
I would get out of my hairt
and aneath the heich lift.
If I could pray.
And ane o aa the starns
maun still be.

154

I think, I ken,
which ane alane
has lastit –
which ane a siller toun
stauns at the end of that beam in the heivens . . .

FROM THE GERMAN OF KURT HEYNICKE

GETHSEMANE

Aa men are Christ.
There's a daurk gairden.
There the cup maun be sipped.
Lord, let it not gae frae us.
Aa of ane luve.
Aa of wersh pain.
Aa seekin to be saved.
Lord, Thy Way is our cross.
Let it not gae frae us.

FROM THE GERMAN OF NELLY SACHS

IN THIS AMETHYST

In this amethyst
are implantit the ages of nicht
and a forkent intelligence of licht
explodes the sadness
which aye flowed
and wept

Your deein aye shines
haurd violet

Peter France

FROM THE RUSSIAN OF ANNA AKHMATOVA

1

YOUTH

My young hands signed
My name on that document
Among stalls selling flowers
And the gramophone's clatter
Under the gas lanterns'
Oblique tipsy stare.
I was older than the century
By exactly ten years.

And the setting sun was shrouded
With white cherries in mourning
Scattering a delicate
Dry and fragrant rain.
And the clouds were shot through
With Tsushima's bloody foam,
And carriages bore smoothly
The corpses of today.

But now that distant evening
Would seem to us a carnival,
Would seem a masquerade,
A fairy-tale *grand-gala*.

Of that house there remains
Not a brick, that alley's felled,
Those hats and shoes retired
Long ago to the museum.
Who knows the sky's emptiness
Where the tower has fallen?
Who knows the house's quietness
Where the son never came home?
You persist like conscience
Or like air, always with me.
But why demand an answer?
Your witnesses I know:
Incandescent with music
The Pavlovsk station dome,
And the Babolov palace's
White-maned cascade.

2

Gold rusts, the sword rusts in the sheath,
And marble crumbles. Death takes all.
The strongest thing on earth is grief,
The longest-lived the word imperial.

FROM THE RUSSIAN OF BORIS PASTERNAK
(with Jon Stallworthy)

MAGDALENE

Each night brings back my demon,
My fee for services rendered.
The memories of sin crowd in
Like vampires sucking at my heart,
Remembering how I surrendered
To men's desires, a crazy tart
Only at home on the boulevard.

A few minutes more and then
The lips of the grave will meet.
But first I will go as far
As I can, and break open
My life, Lord, at Your feet
Like an alabaster jar.

Oh, where now would I be,
My Teacher and Redeemer,
If every night eternity
Were not ensconced in my flat
And waiting like a customer,
Entangled in my net?

But what is the meaning of sin and death
And hell, when everyone can see
Me grafted indissolubly
To You, as a cutting to a tree,
In my immeasurable grief?

And, Jesus, when I press
Your feet against my knees,
Perhaps I am learning already
To hug the square shaft of a cross
And, swooning, I prepare Your body
For other oils than these.

FROM THE RUSSIAN OF GENNADY AIGI

1

JASMINE: FROM EARLY MORNING

but at dawn they gathered
out of mist little islands
of their solemnly-festive August visibility –

fusing ever more clearly in white exhalation
slowly into the Sun – which stood as firm and as near
as their Father's house
entering his chamber in Russian-carpenterly radiance –

in a holy rite

2

YOU-DAY

and reaching especially the hearts of swifts
the wind was light – bearer of gladness:

(yourself you were so much in every place!) –

in shimmering-and-prayer for you
forgiving
Day
reared hugely up! –

in the swifts cried (like a child-soul):

utter-inaccessibility! –

yet in it there was openness – here
as if
from light! –

and hearing was – secretly-still . . . –

(keen – in you – as in the crying)

FROM THE RUSSIAN OF OLEG CHUKHONTSEV

REVEILLE

I

Waking and coming to his senses
painfully, thinking in the dark
here he was, lying by his wife,
though it could have been somebody else's.
and not lying just anywhere,
but his own bed, under the blankets,
only him and the wife, and just think,
a few more and he could be waking
not here, coming to in the dark,
but spreadeagled in some hall-
way, snow-drift, or heaven knows where,
or even not waking at all,
or if he did, not knowing where,
the cooler perhaps, or a station
this time, and thank god he was in bed,
not a bench or a bunk, and them poking
his chest, demanding his name,
identity check, licking fingers,
and how can you explain anything
to anyone . . . and here's this slob
on duty, drinking his tea,
as if he was back home on the farm,
light and warm, a pigeon at the window,
mouth opens, and half the loaf's gone,
he sits there, the pigeon is staring
hungrily, looking, waiting,
will he cough it up? no, not him,
not his style! – and it was so early,
so early in the morning, that it wasn't
from sleep, but from happiness

at waking up in his own bed,
lying there beside the wife,
all in one piece, and what's more
there was liquor still stashed away,
what luck, and no-one had spat
in his soul or his face – and the night
had gone alright, he thought.

II

He's awake, the old tom, thought his wife,
awakened as usual, like a sergeant
on freezing guard at the arsenal
and roused by a whisper or the squeak
of a mouse or the thought of a spy,
and she lay there holding her breath,
Sunday morning, dozing and listening
to him getting up, and knowing
it all in advance, his thoughts,
just one single thought, and even knowing
where the booze was – he'd be behind bars
long ago if it wasn't for her
keeping watch – and angrily listening
to the boom of the taps, her side aching
and she realised, just like her,
some loose washer, but she wouldn't groan
like that tap, and yet not long ago
this artist had taken her out
to a smart eating place, a real man,
not a layabout, and gave her flowers
and kept saying, you've a nice figure,
let me draw you in the nude – naked
what of it! but she like a fool
chickened out: what's wrong with you then
all goggle eyed, never seen a woman?
men, what they've come to: alcoholics
or perverts, my God, it's enough
to turn a woman off, and her moiling
and toiling and inching and pinching,
and come night time the same old visions . . .
oranges tumbling into her lap,
and the girl is expecting – but why? –
and bang, she's awake, what a nightmare:
no wonder she felt a bit shaky,
she's only thirteen and that scrounger
up to the gunwales in drink
might fall into her bed, and that's it,

why can't somebody take him in hand?
it's a vale of tears, says his mother,
and the worst is, she's right, the old fool.

III

This year they've all been talking
about happiness and world peace –
it struck her as she lay there dozing –
but last year they didn't so much,
it means war, says grandma, and crosses
herself, and drives mummy so mad
she's started to get palpitations,
but I love the Sunday programmes,
you eat your salami sandwich
and some fellow with a balalaika
dances and sings on the screen,
I really like literature, the sort
that turns you on, open-air readings,
people crammed in like sardines,
and floodlights, and poets, jam pies
at eleven kopecks a time –
one kopeck is for the Olympics –
on comes this guy, stylish sweater,
me sitting there holding my pie,
he starts shaking, one hand on the mike,
and the white snow comes drifting from heaven,
and the words are so lovely, so sweet
you've a lump in your throat, and I
didn't twig for a while it was cabbage,
but who wants to eat when the stadium
is buzzing – the speaker was right,
men and women are made to be happy
he said, as a bird is for flight,
it makes you think: I'm in luck
and maybe I'm happy, who knows,
yes I'm happy; daddy goes drinking
and mummy keeps scolding, I fly,
I fling out my arms and I swim,
only dreaming of course, but in school
they said you can really take off
if you concentrate all your willpower,
and sometimes I go on the balcony,
it's scary, but a mystical voice
says fly, and I can hear ringing,
one step, then another, then half . . .

IV

Forgive thy poor ignorant servant,
forgive me, old fool that I am,
putting out the bottle of polish
by mistake for his horrible booze,
was it my fault or was it the devil's?
have pity on foolish Matryona,
half asleep he groped in his boot,
my boy, and his wife just walked out,
slammed the door – but why? and where to?
leaving home, or going to get beer?
bestow, I beseech thee, thy patience
on all men, and save the impatient,
the godless, the sheep gone astray,
who're too good for their mothers and homes,
the old and the young, we are all
in thy keeping, harden not thy heart,
nor leave us crammed in here with no icons,
as it is, I'm ashamed with strangers:
Matryona, just pop in at the council
and show them your invalid card –
I beseech thee, give ear to my tears,
I don't ask thy help for myself,
my days have vanished like smoke
and my bones are consumed like ashes,
I beseech thee, do not abandon
wives and husbands, take care of the children,
keep those who thirst from the bottle,
and give to the drinkers their tears
as the hair of the dog, and if here
we have sinned, thou shalt smite us with thunder;
and what we have sowed with our sorrow
we shall reap in gladness hereafter.

FROM THE RUSSIAN OF JOSEPH BRODSKY

1

ALMOST AN ELEGY

In days gone by I too would stand and wait
under the columns of the Stock Exchange
for the cold rain to stop. And I believed
it was God's gift. I was happy once. I lived
a prisoner of angels. Rode out against monsters.
Like Jacob I would stand at the main door
lying in wait until a certain girl
came running down the stairs.
                              All this has gone
somewhere for good. All disappeared. And yet
I look out of the window and I write
"somewhere" and after "where" no question mark.
September now. Before me lies a garden.
The thunder's distant rumble fills my ears.
In the dense foliage the full ripe pears
hang down like emblems of virility.
And as a miser lets his relatives
into his kitchen only, now my ears admit
only the downpour to my slumbering mind:
not music yet, already more than noise.

2

17th SONNET TO MARY QUEEN OF SCOTS

The thing that dragged from English mouths a shout
of wonderment, and that impels
my own mouth with its taste for rouge
to blasphemy, that could compel
Philip to tear his face from Art
and order an Armada to set sail,
it was – I can't complete the big
build-up of phrases – well, your wig,
lying fallen from your fallen head
(evil eternity), it seemed
your one and only bow, and though
it may not have provoked a fight
among spectators, even so
it brought your enemies to their feet.

Robin Fulton

FROM THE NORWEGIAN OF OLAV H. HAUGE

1

THE STONE GOD

You carry the stone god
within you.
You give him loyal service
and secret offerings.
Wreaths and lit candles
you bring him
with bloody hands,
yet still feel
the coldness of him
in your heart,
know your breath
hardens like his
and your smile
as chilled.

2

MANY YEARS' EXPERIENCE
WITH BOW AND ARROW

It's the black dot right
in the middle you're to hit,
right there, where
the arrow will stand trembling!
But just there is where you don't hit.
You're close, closer, no,
not close enough.
So it's off to pick the arrows up,
walk back, try again.
The black dot teases you.
Until you understand the arrow
that stands there trembling:
here too is a mid-point.

3

PAUL CELAN

Shut inside this rotating
ghost-house, life,
with little openings each
giving on
its own reality
– we live,
are at home here –
most of us gather
at the biggest one,
this is the world,
we say.

At yours
sat
only you –
eye black
diamond,
heart
a bloodstone.

FROM THE SWEDISH OF ÖSTEN SJÖSTRAND

1

IN THE BEGINNING, STILL

Musée de l'Homme, Paris

I see the jawbone,
the jaw cavity where a tongue once formed
wheezing call notes, a strange speech –

I see the teeth,
the small eye-teeth which once tore apart
a fledgling, a poor leveret
snared in the dry
European savanna grass –

I see the cranium,
a flat brain pan which sur-
rounded what thoughts?

165

All at once, at my side, among the ruins,
I see the patient writer –
and the horsemen, the thick-necked, the scarred,
in worn hides – their subtle flights
    sure ambushes: the pyramids
    of human heads, crania:
    in 1238, 1398 –

Dead, living: so close, so close –

Only a few steps from me, in the throng,
    I hear a mercenary say,
    out of the depths of the whole human race:
    Lord –
    I am not worthy that you should enter
    under my roof.

2

THOUGHTS BEFORE A PAPAL GALLEY

Justice: this fugitive from the Victorious camp . . .

I

"The Truth shall make you free –"

"That truth was truth
for the few. The high ideals were the wall,
the frieze, hiding the knife-stabs of the mighty,
the dirty political slaughter . . .
The chain-smiths! The light-forgers!
Those who were almost shadowless. Oppression's

defenders . . . When the light now changes owners
they will all plunge down
the slopes of oblivion.
Like the image of Falsehood which they raised
in flesh and bronze on some exalted place."

II

Now are silent . . . Up from the open cabin,
the tabernacle, the Prince, the Commander
surveyed, inspected, surrounded by cupids
and heraldic beasts, the living
tools . . . Yes, the truth freed few
from the neck-iron, the foot-iron.

III

With bull-heads, fish-bodies, snake-legs,
with the snake-heads they fought,
they made assaults, they were trampled down:
also those who fled, those who could do no more,
those who turned away, they were trampled down,
they were crushed under the hooves. Thrust down

in their animal trance, their dungeon
by an overwhelming, light-enfolded enemy . . .

But hands which were once stretched in impotence
could now throw the very rock to the height,
raise the earth out of its orbit. No weapons,
no walls, could check the rising army
which now claimed justice for man-slave
and woman-slave, the living tools –

With my hand touching the wall fragments
I felt the storm wind's purpose with the last
visible remains of the Acropolis,
the crusader castle. Under the trees boys
and girls boxed, relentlessly silent,
or chattering, against their own shadows.

IV

The superior things, the tyrants,
the heraldic beasts, are reduced
by an execution squad . . . Under
a fig tree's living branches
I saw (in dream) a galaxy
of embryonic worlds, a horse

rearing for a new
arrogant leap . . . And the sea went on
surging in the distance, remotely. But,
I saw more! On the slope of the Acropolis,
in the slanting light, I saw
the goddess with clipped wings, Nike Apteros,
freed from the fetters of injustice . . .
In the mountains, high above Ephesos,
I met, before the red light
before the image of the Godmother, an Armenian
construction engineer. Together we approached
Panayía Kapulu . . . Above our heads
roared a jet from Asia or
from Europe.

3

THE NECESSARY ANTISTROPHES

The sun rises
over graves on both sides of the border.
    The rain falls
over people on both sides of the border.
    The air
those still living breathe, I also breathe –
    I accept.
Like the air. Like the living water.

    Turned
to the apse of silence, I see them vanish,
    the perishable
seductive images, the photographs,
    the worn
reproductions, the projections . . .

    Turned
towards silence, I see the earth that bears us
    vanish,
the movements of the bodies, the visible particles,
    the furious struggle
in the sea-depths, and the victories on the beaches
    vanish –

I am neither for nor against. I renounce
   the outer, the inner
instant images of evil and good,
   the scarce time's
power constellations. God himself, not thinking
   about God
grants peace . . .

   This banished
evil-doer has something important to tell me.
   This
criminal, detested by all, has perhaps
   a message
to bring – I hear the ultrasonic knife
   in the doctor's hand . . .

The fragile is the only solid –
   in the night
where the sun still hesitates in people
   who are breathing:
on both sides of the Wall.

FROM THE SWEDISH OF TOMAS TRANSTRÖMER

1

IZMIR AT THREE O'CLOCK

Just ahead in the almost empty street
two beggars, one without legs –
he's carried on the other one's back.

They stood – as on a midnight road an animal
stands blinded staring into the carlights –
for one moment before passing on

and scuttled across the street like boys
in a playground while the midday heat's
myriad of clocks ticked in space.

Blue flowed past on the waters, flickering.
Black crept and shrank, stared from stone.
White blew up to a storm in the eyes.

When three o'clock was trampled under hooves
and darkness pounded in the wall of light
the city lay crawling at the sea's door

gleaming in the vulture's telescopic sight.

2

THE HALF-FINISHED HEAVEN

Despondency breaks off its course.
Anguish breaks off its course.
The vulture breaks off its flight.

The eager light streams out,
even the ghosts take a draught.

And our paintings see daylight,
our red beasts of the ice-age studios.

Everything begins to look around.
We walk in the sun in hundreds.

Each man is a half open door
leading to a room for everyone.

The endless ground under us.

The water is shining among the trees.

The lake is a window into the earth.

3

THE OUTPOST

I'm ordered out in a heap of stones
like a distinguished corpse from the iron age.
The others are back in the tent sleeping
stretched out like spokes in a wheel.

In the tent the stove rules: a big snake
that has swallowed a ball of fire and hisses.
But out in the spring night it is silent
among cold stones that are waiting for day.

Out there in the cold I begin to fly
like a shaman, I fly to her body
with its white marks from her bikini –
we were out in the sun. The moss was warm.

I flit over warm moments
but can't stop for long.
They're whistling me back through space –
I crawl out from the stones. Here and now.

Mission: to be where I am.
Even in that ridiculous, deadly serious
role – I am the place
where creation is working itself out.

Daybreak, the sparse tree-trunks
are coloured now, the frost-bitten
spring flowers form a silent search party
for someone who has vanished in the dark.

But to be where I am. And to wait.
I am anxious, stubborn, confused.
Coming events, they're there already!
I know it. They're outside:

a murmuring crowd outside the gate.
They can pass only one by one.
They want in. Why? They're coming
one by one. I am the turnstile.

4

WINTER'S GAZE

I lean like a ladder and with my face
reach in to the second floor of the cherry tree.
I'm inside the bell of colours, it chimes with sunlight.
I polish off the swarthy red berries faster than four magpies.

A sudden chill, from a great distance, meets me.
The moment blackens
and remains like an axe-cut in a tree-trunk.

From now on it's late. We make off half-running
out of sight, down, down in the ancient sewage system.
The tunnels. We walk about there for months
half in service and half in flight.

Brief devotions when some hatchway opens above us
and a weak light falls.
We look up: the starry sky through the grating.

5

VERMEER

No protected world . . . Just behind the wall the noise begins,
the inn is there
with laughter and bickering, rows of teeth, tears, the din of bells
and the deranged brother-in-law, the death-bringer we all must
    tremble for.

The big explosion and the tramp of rescue arriving late
the boats preening themselves on the straits, the money creeping down
    in the wrong man's pocket
demands stacked on demands
gaping red flowerheads sweating premonitions of war.

In from there and right through the wall into the clear studio
into the second that's allowed to live for centuries.
Pictures that call themselves "The Music Lesson"
or "Woman in Blue Reading a Letter" –
she's in her eighth month, two hearts kicking inside her.
On the wall behind is a crumpled map of Terra Incognita.

Breathe calmly . . . An unknown blue material nailed to the chairs.
The gold studs flew in with incredible speed
and stopped abruptly
as if they had never been other than stillness.

Ears sing, from depth or height.
It's the pressure from the other side of the wall
it makes each fact float
and steadies the brush.

172

It hurts to go through walls, it makes you ill
but it is necessary.
The world is one. But walls . . .
And the wall is part of yourself –
we know or we don't know, but it's true for us all
except for small children. No walls for them.

The clear sky has leant itself against the wall.
It's like a prayer to the emptiness.
And the emptiness turns its face to us
and whispers
"I am not empty, I am open."

Tessa Ransford

FROM THE GERMAN OF J. C. F. HÖLDERLIN

1

MY PORTION

The Autumn is at rest in its fulness now
And purified the grape, and the orchard red
   With fruit, though many lovely blossoms
      Fell down to earth with a thankful gesture.

In fields around I stroll along quiet paths
And see how those who wait with content win their
   Reward, and gladly reap the blessing
      Yielded to people who toil to earn it.

Soft light is palely filtered through branching trees
To share out joy, provided for working folk;
   For not by hand of Man alone do
      Fruits come to harvest beneath the heavens.

And do you shine for me in your radiance too,
And blow for me, friendly breeze? And seem
   To bless the joy I used to have, by
      Hovering round as if I were lucky?

So was I once; yet fading as roses was
That goodly life, alas! And the gracious stars
   Repeatedly remind me of it,
      Lasting for ever in their florescence.

And blest is he who lives with his faithful wife
At peace beside his hearth in a righteous land.
   The sun shines brighter, firmer the earth for
      Those who are safely, securely rooted.

Unlike a plant, with roots in its patch of ground,
My mortal soul is scorched in the heat of day
   And wanders aimless, in poverty,
      Over the hallowed earth, bewildered.

Too powerfully, ethereal heights, you draw
Me up, amid the storms, and on clearer days
   I feel your ebb and flow consume me
      Free-roaming, infinite, godly forces.

But now today I'll tread the old pathway toward
The grove where golden treetops adorn themselves
   With dying foliage: you favourite
     Memories, crown even me with garlands!

To save my human heart and establish me
Like others, in some settled condition too,
   So that my soul need not be ever
     Homeless and soaring beyond this life-time,

Let song become my sanctuary, friendly source
Of blessing; garden tended by me with care
   Where I may wander through the flowers
     Knowing them such as will never wither,

And dwell secure in trustful simplicity
When racing Time outside in his whirling strength
   Destructively is heard, whereas the
     Sun with more gentleness bears upon me.

You bless with kindness all of us mortal ones,
O powers of Heaven, and give to each one his part.
   O bless e'en mine, nor let the Fates too
     Soon put an end to my dreams and poems.

2

ACHILLES

Magnificent son of the gods! When you lost your beloved
You strode to the beach and wept aloud to the flood
Until your cry was engulfed in the sacred ocean-bed
And your heart in the silence; where from noise of the fleet,
Distant, deep below waves, in a peaceful grotto blue-
Hazed Thetis lived, princess of the sea, who protected you.
She was the young man's mother, and powerful goddess she –
Who once had lovingly taken the boy to a rocky part
Of her island and suckled him, to the pounding roar of the breakers
And by such bold bathing fashioned him into a hero.
And his mother took in the youth's bitter lamenting,
Arose from the sea-bed sorrowfully in mist,
Calmed with tender embrace her darling one,
And he listened, as she soothingly promised to help.

175

Son of the gods! If I were as you, then I could share
My secret sorrow trustingly with an immortal one.
It cannot be: I must endure the insult as if
I never belonged to her, who thinks of me with tears.
Kindly gods! You hear the beseeching of every man,
Ah! And inwardly I've honoured you, holy Light,
All my life, and you, Earth, with fountains and woods;
And Father Aether, I've felt you bless and purify
My heart; – gracious ones, O mitigate my pain,
That the soul within me should not too soon be put to silence,
That I may live, and give to you, high, heavenly powers,
A song of thankful praise as day at last departs,
Grateful for previous blessings, delights of bygone youth:
And then favour me, raise me up in my loneliness.

Donald Campbell

FROM THE RUSSIAN OF VLADIMIR MAYAKOVSKY

Aw You . . .
Ye werenae feart!
Ye came
determined
set
undaunted
(a female Abednego!)
intil the flames
the fiery furnace
o my coorse
and angry life.

Ye limmer!
Ye looked straucht
intil the ee
o my hurricane
saw
what nane ither
had seen afore
– the hert
ahint the flamin lowe
the fear
ablow the bleezin roar.

The ither quines
(Ladies o the toun!
Speirin spinsters aa!)
thocht ye a ferlie
cried ye "whore"
"Love sic a loon?
Thon keelie tyke?
She maun be mad!
Afore
she kens
he'll ding her doun!"

But you?
What were ye like?
Ye didnae gie a jot
– just grabbed my hert
and gart it stot!

Douglas Dunn

FROM THE ITALIAN OF GIACOMO LEOPARDI

TO HIMSELF

Exhausted heart, illimitable rest
Shall be yours now. Illusion's activist,
I broke belief in it, and now I want
Nothing, the darling or the fraudulent.
Stilled beat, be easy; nothingness annuls
Pity. Life is no more than and no less
Than sordid tedium and bitterness.
It is not worthy of your lively pulse,
Your worried sympathy. The world is filth:
Withdraw your pity from its commonwealth.
Fate's only gift to us is that we die –
Self-mockery, therefore; mock Nature, curse
Infinite vanity, and vilify
Nature that rules with pain and secret force.

FROM THE POLISH OF PIOTR SOMMER

1

BETWEEN BUS-STOP AND HOME

(To Pawel and Helena)

You go to visit your friend after a film-show,
and your wife is left alone at home
and your mother, you're beginning to think about
when you've stepped off the bus, is in another town,
ill, and yesterday you had a telegram from her.
Between the stop on the 140A bus route
and your friend's home (passing, that is,
a closed shop, buying cigarettes
in the kiosk, before the house and even in the lift),
before you enter his flat and begin
evening conversation with him and his wife, you're alone.
Your son went to your wife's parents yesterday
and is alone without you and without his mother.
You think about all this before the door's opened
as snow powders straight into your face
though it's the third decade of March, pacing out

178

this short-distance between bus-stop and house.
Suddenly you pay attention to this routine loneliness
as if opposed to yourself
as if resisting those you are thinking about.

2

TWO GESTURES

A woman drags herself from bed.
You know, I think I ought to make myself some dinner.
But she doesn't have time
and dies between
two gestures: her mother's,
and her child's, never discovering
who she belonged to more.

Alexander Hutchison

FROM THE LATIN OF CATULLUS

Noo, Eppie, ye've lat doon yer freens
Ye've lat me doon tee, an we wis lik breethers.

Is this the wye the warl works noo – nae trust
or nithin? Is this fit ye think the pooers abeen
tik a reed-rosy shine til?

It seems that wye. A'm left t' fend for masel.
Fit can fowk dee? Faa's left t' rely on?

A wis taen richt in, coortit, cossetit.
Noo aa yer courtesies, aa yer fine wirdies
are nithin bit vapour, a parcel a ween
an you a vanishin vapour tee.

Ach, awa – though ye dinna mine, the Gods'll nae
forget: ye'll git a recknin yet fae Faith hersel.

FROM THE FRENCH OF PIERRE DE RONSARD

SONNETS

1

These lang dreich nichts, fan the Meen's
a traichlin traal gaun roon sae sweir,
fan the bantie's blate t' gie 's a cockle-daw,
fan mirk for ivry sowel sair-deen's rax't oot a year –
A micht've dwined athoot yon unco freen,
that dodged richt roon t' swage ma stoonin hert,
an settl't bare as licht in my airm-span,
t' sing sae douce o blithe an lees.
Nae doot ye're prood an coorse an caal;
bit in seclusion fine a hae yer tween.
Yon bonny bogle coories doon sae swack:
alangside her a stan or tak ma ease.
Nithin's ivver been held back.
Syne sleep's the salve that chaets the deepest dool.
Fan love deals oot yer haun deception's
trumps – nae herts – exception maks the rule.

2

Since she's hale winter, nithin bit ice,
aa snaw, an her hairt birsels wi spikes an ice,
an only ma sangs tak her likin ataa,
fit wye am I here besottit – an nae awa?
Her name, her faimly, fit is it t' me
bit bondage – rigged fancy – that gran pedigree?
Lass, a'm nae sae grey or bald or saft
that some ither, warm-hertit, quidna clim t' ma laft.
Love's a bairn that's nivver gainsaid.
Ye're nae sae prood or weel arrayed
that ye can spurn strachtforrit hairt's affection.
Blithe spring's awa – it winna tak direction –
bit loo me noo for my scant hair,
an a'll catch yer haun fan it trimmles at the stair.

3

Aabody says, Sandy, she's nae ataa
lik fit ye said. A widna ken.
A'm aff ma heed. It's nithin t' dee wi me.
A canna tell if she's funcy or if she's plain.
Aa them that're coortin wyse an clivver
                (chasin efter somethin snooty)
quidna be richt smitten ivver –
A coortin loon's a bap: quidna sup ees brose
at brakfast (if love's as glyte as they say).
Bit seekin efter perfect beauty canna be
as daft as that – aabody wints it –
raither somethin cunnin, canny
                (taks a lad that's aye on duty)
taks a chiel that kens fits fit.
Bit that's nae for me t' say –
                (a'm that doazent)
blin an feel – day's nicht; nicht, day.
The thristle's ivry bit as bonny as the rose.

4

Fan I cam back (faith, a'm still lackin sleep)
the kiss a got wis lik frost on a neep –
caal, nae relish, lik a deid man's haun:
a kiss lik her breether got fae chaste Diane,
or lik some granny gies til her favourite quine,
or a fiancee doles oot fan her man taes the line.
Naither juicy, nor tasty, nor nithin ataa.
His ma lip gane as bitter as aa that, wee cra?
Weel, ye'll jist hae t' ging t' tak lessons wi doos:
aa lovey-dovey on stumps or heich boos.
Wi their wee beakies tit-tittin lang an fine.
On bendit knee a'm implorin ye, quine,
for slabbery kisses (richt up t' the hilt)
                             fan we jine thegither;
or leav't weel alane (nae marra intil't)
                             til warmer wither.

FROM THE FRENCH OF RAYMOND QUENEAU

Deef the mirk, the shadda, the haar,
deef the birk, the cassay-stane;
deef the haimmer t' the anvil-heid,
deef the sea, the houlat his lane.

Blin the bumlick, blin the mirk,
blin the girss, the barley-heid;
blin the mowdie aneth the grun,
blin the roddan, blin the seed.

Dumb the mirk, the deepest dool,
dumb the sangs, an dumb the laich;
dumb the glimmer o the lift,
dumb the wid, the watter, the craik.

The hale hypothec's totteran noo:
totteran baists, totteran stanes;
totteran tee the likeness drawn,
a totteran yaff t' shift yer banes.

Bit faa glisks, faa kens,
faa spiks a wird o't yet?

Roderick Watson

FROM RUSSIAN OF ANDREI VOZNESENSKY

1

FOGGY STREET

Street as rookie as a doo.
                    Like corks, policemen bide.
Mirk aa through.
Whatna century am I at? Whatna ill tide?

Aathing's disjaskit like some fell dwaum.
                    Fowk dwine and mell.
I glaum.
Or trauchle, mair like, i cotton wool.

Nebs. Bonnets. Car-lichts blur.
                    Like a lantren-shaw they breenge and twine.
Yer galoshes, sir?
And dinnae forget yer heid this time!

It's like a wumman wha's barely quit your mou
                    but brairds, swithered
awa frae luve – a wedo,
                    aye yours – abies anither's.

I tummle pedestrians and chapp on stanes,
                    Venus? An ice-cream kiosk!
Freens?
Ach, thae couthy Iagos!

Yersel?! Chitterin in a coat that's tashed,
                    staundin alane and lost, my dear!
– Moustached?!
Wi hoar-frost in yon hairy ear!

I trauchle, dwaible, haud on by,
                    haar, haar – there's naething clear,
wha's cheek, in the haar, are you brushin noo?
Hi!
Haar, haar – ye dinna get through. . . .

But man! Whan the mirk turns blue, schire!

2

PARABOLIC BALLAD

Oor weird, like a rocket, taks a parabola
Maistly in mirk, but whiles on a watergaw.

Fiery Gauguin the reid-heided penter,
A richt bohemian – was yince a stockbroker.
Tae faa til the royal Louvre
                         frae oot o Montmartre,
He screivit
         an arc
                 through Java and Sumatra!

He juist took-aff, leavin the coofs tae queue for gowd,
The cluckin o wives, Academy guff,
And pu'd awa
              frae the pu o the Earth.

The savants snichered intil their beer:
"The straucht line's clear, parabola's owre sheer,
Mair wice tae heed the foot-rule o paradise!"

Like a goustrous rocket he blasted aff, wi a gale
That flypit their claw-hemmer coats and lugs,
An cam til the Louvre, no by the hall –
But ram-stam
            parabola
                bashed-in the ceiling!

Ilk ane drees his ain weird
A sclater – its crack, man – on a camsteerie arc.

A lassie used tae bide by oor stairs
We studied thegither, sat the exams.
But whaur did I get til!
                 taen awa wi the deil
Tae the creeshie ambiguous starns o the Sooth!

Ye maun forgie me yon daft parabola.
Your wee shouders were frozen in the oorie close
O but ye dirled i the mirk o the Universe
Trim and trig, like an aerial rod!
I'm fleein yet,
            but brocht back tae land –
Earthy and cauld by your callin,
Ach, this parabola is no sae easy dreed!

Lauchin at laws, symposiums, prognoses,
Art,
    love,
        and history
Birl in on a parabolic coorse!

He's set for the salt-mines richt awa.

The straught line's aiblins shorter – efter aa?

3

SELF-PORTRAIT

He's as skinny as a sauch. Collie-faced and wantin a shave.
Three nichts his banes
              hae gar'd my maittress creak.
His shaddaw hings tae the waa like a swee.
The mou blaws smoke, syne's up in a lowe.

"C'awa, c'awa," he crochles, "Ma wee Ruskie pomes.
The dirk he'll hae, or aiblins a gun?
A genius ye say? Or whiles a cynic on the fence
that minds the steer, but bides his fun?

Aye, or sall we slaver tae the T.L.S. and straucht
turn oot oor benmaist hert like a roll-yer-ain?"

But why does he buss you tae my face?
Why does he try my muffler on?
And glower ahint my fag-end's aiss?

Gie owre, gie owre!
S.O.S!

Robin Bell

FROM THE FRENCH OF JEANNE MAILLET
(with Maria Blasquez)

FOUR POEMS

1

I want to be part of the place
where willow branches recall the basket's weave.
I want to be part of the moment
where the hand gives its blessing to the tortured withy.

2

When love came to touch her
the rock took on its beauty
. . . in an instant the fountainhead was born . . .

3

If you want
we can make it from the vaults, no tracing records,
a sunbeam making up the sea,
holding hands on a white tablecloth,
just a little to nourish our story,
and our love
free from the power
of names . . .

4

Do you hear the wind? Pardon my presumption
of looking beyond the trickling hour-glass.
That's how I live! Daring to set out at dawn
where almond blossom shines upon the grass.

Valerie Gillies

FROM THE ITALIAN OF DANTE ALIGHIERI

From *PURGATORIO, CANTO 26*
(Dante talks to the spirits of the poets, Guido Guinicelli
and Arnaut Daniel)

And I walked without hearing or speaking a word,
    deep in thought, and gazing at him a long while;
    because of the flames, I came no closer than I dared.
Once I had feasted my eyes on him, I offered
    myself, ready to be at his service,
    with the vow that inspires faith in others.
And he said to me, "What I hear you say
    leaves such a trace in me, so clear
    as Lethe cannot blur or wash away.
But if your oath just now was truly sincere,
    tell me, what's the reason that you show
    when you speak, or look, you hold me dear?"
I answered, "It's the sweet speech you link
    in verse which, as long as the modern style lasts,
    must make precious its very ink."
"O brother," he said, "I can show you one"
    – and he pointed to a spirit in front –
    "who was a better craftsman of his mother-tongue.
Love-poems or prose romances, he altogether
    surpasses everybody, so let the fools yap
    who think the bard of Limoges is better.
They turn more to what they hear, than to the way
    of truth, and they fix their opinion
    before considering what art or reason have to say.
In the old days, many did so with Guittone,
    the loud-mouths praised him louder until
    truth taught most of them what was phoney.
Now, if you have such high privilege
    that you are allowed to go into the cloister
    where Christ is abbot of the college,
Say for me there one 'Our Father',
    so far as we of this world need your help,
    since it's not in our power to sin further."
Maybe to make room for others who pressed on
    close to him, he vanished through the flame
    as through deep water a fish moves and is gone.
I went forward to the soul he'd shown before,
    and said I wished to know his name,
    desiring to write it in a place of honour.
And at once he started to say freely:

"Yir courtassy sae pleases me, aye whan ye're speirin
I cuidna, widna lig in derne frae ye:
I am hecht Arnaut, whae greets and gaes singin.
I think on yon that langsyne wes sae fuilitch,
an see afore me joy, in joy I'm howpin.
Noo I wis ye, bi yon grace
bi which ye win awa abune the heuch turn-gree,
whiles mind on me, wha gets his paiks."
Then he hid himself in their fiery refinery.

Ronald Butlin

FROM THE SPANISH OF LUIS CERNUDA

THE CITY CEMETERY

There are open railings and walls
and black earth and no trees and no grass
and wooden benches where old people sit
the whole afternoon without speaking.
All around there are tenements and shops.
The children play in streets and the trains
rattle past the graves. It is a poor district.

As if patching-up some piece of grey material, rain
-sodden rags hang across the windows.
The writing on the tombstones is unreadable, and anyway
for the last two hundred years they have been burying not men
but corpses without friends even to forget them, dead
secrets. But when the sun blazes for those few days
around June, surely the old bones down there feel something.

No leaf, no bird. Nothing but stone. Earth.
Is Hell like this? Pain and more pain, clamour,
misery, a chill that seeps everywhere freezing
everything; and the dead are not left in peace,
for life goes about its business here like a prostitute
who works only under the cover of darkness.

When the dirty evening twilight smears the sky
and the factory smoke falls back down
as grey ash, people are shouting in the pubs;
and then a train passes,
its echoes stretching the sounds like a trumpet's snarl.

– But not for Judgement Day. You have no names now,
so be at peace; if you can sleep, then sleep.
For even God may be forgetting you.

FROM THE FRENCH OF JULES SUPERVIELLE

1

THE NEIGHBOURING ROOM

Turn your back on this man
but do not leave him,
(let your glance fall elsewhere
in its confusion and cruelty),
remain with him and remain silent
for he can hardly tell daylight from darkness,
nor whether it is the ever-circling heavens
or his heart's relentless beat
that torments him.
Put out those lights and you will see his veins shine!
When he stretches out his hand
see how the darkness breathes precious stones there,
glittering even to his finger-tips.
Leave him alone on his bed
where the days and years shall care for him,
and the nights shall keep him terrified
listening to each silence between heartbeats.
Let no-one enter the room
for an enormous dog will be let loose
from there; and having no memory
it will range across all continents
and oceans of the world
seeking the man it left behind
motionless, held fast
in his own hands' grip, glittering
and perfect
even to his finger-tips.

FROM THE FRENCH OF JACQUES DUPIN

1

URN

Forever watching for a second darkness
that will douse this clear and chilling flame
burning without ash.

And the urn that remained empty
we furiously filled with earth,
but it caught fire,
blazing as a beacon for whoever's still to come.

2

EGYPTIAN WOMAN

You would not survive a second birth,
so I carried your breath in a sway of reeds
deep into the desert
to flower for me alone.

But they followed us there:
and that I would be immortal in their name only
they have sealed even these doors with their magic.

Robert Calder

FROM THE RUSSIAN OF OSIP MANDELSTAM

HE WHO HAS FOUND A HORSESHOE

We look at a forest and say it's
a forest of masts, of ships,
red pines,
clear of their shaggy burden, clear to the top
should, in the storm, creak
like single pine-trees
in air's treeless ragings.
The plumbline, fixed fast
to the dancing deck under the salt heel
of the wind, will hold, as the seafarer,
forever thirsting for distance, trails
through furrows of water the geometer's
fragile instruments to register,
against the earth's bosom pulling,
the sea's rough surfaces.

But still, breathing tears of resin
which seep from the ship's timbers,
observing with reverence
riveted boards set in bulkheads
(not by Bethlehem's craftsman
but by that other carpenter, father
of wanderings, friend of the seafarer)
we see
these also stood once on firm earth
uneasy as a donkey's vertebral column,
tops oblivious of roots,
on the spur of a greatly-famous mountain,
soughed under sweet rainstorms
and offered in vain their great burden to the skies
for a pinch of salt.

Where to start?
It all pitches, shivers, cracks.
Air shakes with similes.
No word's better than any other;
earth hums with metaphors,
carts harnessed to shimmering flocks
of birds all straining together
speeding
racing against the race-track favourites.

Thrice blest the man who sets a name in his song.
A song a name graces
outlasts all others –
She may among her companions be known by the headband
which saves her from fainting at such strong smells,
of either the nearness of man,
the fur of a powerful animal or simply
the scent of spice rubbed between hands.

Sometime's air's dark as water and all in it
swims like fish
which weaves a way through the sphere,
dense, flexible, scarcely warm,
crystal in which wheels move and horses shy,
and Naeara's moist black soil that's turned over afresh
each night with pitchforks, shovels, mattocks, ploughs.
Air's as profoundly mingled as earth is;
you can't escape it, can scarce get into it.

Rustling runs through trees as through lush grasses.
Children are playing knucklebones with bits of animals' backbones.
The delicate accounting of our age is near complete.
For what there was, thanks:
I also made my mistakes, got lost, buried in the accounts.
The age rang out like a golden globe
seamless and hollow, held up by nobody.
When touched it responded "yes" and "no"
as a child answers
"I'll give you an apple", or, "won't",
its face an exact match of its voice's intonation.

The sound goes on though its cause is gone.
The horse snorts in lather in the dust
though the keen curve of its neck recalls
legs extended racing,
not only four
but as many as the stones
on the road
coming to life four at a time
with each bound of the burning racehorse.

So
he who has found a horseshoe
blows off the dust, rubs
it with steel wool till it shines
then
hangs it over the door
to rest
and no more strike sparks.
Human lips
   with nothing else to say
keep the shape from the last word said
and the arm still feels the weight
even after the jug
    splashed half the water away
       on the way home.

It's not me that's saying what I'm saying now.
It's dug out of earth like fossilised grains of wheat.
Some have
   on their coins lions
others
  a head;
all sorts of bits of gold, brass, bronze
lie equally honoured in earth.
The age strove to bite through them and left its toothmarks.
Time is biting me like a coin
and now there's not enough of me left even for myself.

Tom Hubbard

FROM THE POLISH OF ADAM MICKIEWICZ
(with Janina Rak)

THE LYART LAIRD

(A Ukrainian Ballant)

The laird rins up fae bour ti tour
    Pechin an tremmlin sair:
He harls the curtain o the bed –
    His young bride bydesna there.

He twynes a straun o his lyart baird
    An glowers ti the groun;
His thochts are daurk as they are deep
    Whan he cries fir his sairvant loun.

"Hei, skellum, why stauns nae dug nor man
    On guaird bi the orchard yett?
Fesh me my bag o the brockie's hide,
    An twa guns, withoutin let."

They draw in dern up ti the hedge
    That girds the arbour roun;
They spy a whiteness throu the mirk –
    A leddy in her goun.

Her ae haun's happin her een wi her hair
    An her breist wi her mantie's bord;
Her ither haun's haudin aff fae her lap
    The airms o a kneelin lawd.

He presses forrit ti her knees:
    "My luve, you leave me nocht;
Your ilka souch, your airms' enbrace
    The lyart laird has bocht.

"It's I hae luved you lang an sair,
    And aye my hert's ableeze –
He's won you wi his wheengin weys
    An his bagfou o bawbees.

"It's ilka nicht he'll sink him doun
    Ti your souple body there,
An he sall pree fae your cramasie lips
    Whit I sall pree nae mair.

"It's I hae rade throu skirl an skail
  As the cauld mune kests her licht;
Fir nocht cuid keep your leman lawd
  Fae biddin this lest guidnicht."

Fae aa his whusperins an mair
  She turned awa her face,
Begood ti greet: then, in a dwam,
  She fell ti his enbrace.

Nou laird an sairvant hae bade lang
  Sae hidlins an sae near:
This nicht sall see anither tryst
  As they graith their deidlie gear.

"O maister, I am sudden crazed,
  That I canna kill thon quean;
My verra gun is in the grup
  o my fivver an my pine."

"You wratch, I'll learn you hou ti greet!
  Lade this wappen here, an then –
Aither blaw oot the harns o that hure
  Or else blaw oot your ain.

"Byde anerlie fir my shot ti tell
  Hou her paramour has fared . . ."
But the sairvant-chiel bade nocht ava
  An fired – at the heid o the laird.

FROM THE FRENCH OF GEORGES RODENBACH

Watter o the auld canals, gaun dowie an donnert,
Sae dreich, i the mids o deid touns, alang the dykes
Buskit wi trees an corbie-steps, raw efter raw
Scarce tracit i this puir watter,
Watter sae auld-like an mauchtless: watter sae peelie-wallie,
Wi nae mair smeddum ti set agin the souch
That runkles it sair . . . Ach! but this waefu watter
Gangs greetin unner the bleck brigs, an maks mane
Fir the shaddas it maun cairry – watter richt liege,
Ti whilk their images are an unmuivin fraucht.
Yit, weirin on an on, at the skimmerin face
It tynes its reflections, as we wad tyne remembrance,

196

An taigles thaim ti haizie miragies.
Watter sae doolie that you'd cry it mortal,
Whit fir sae sterk, aareadies dwyned ti nocht;
Whit fir thae dwams an dreams that turn sae wairsh;
– Nae ti be mair nor a fauselike gless o frost
Whaur the mune hersel is fasht ti be alive?

Christopher Whyte

FROM THE GERMAN OF RAINER MARIA RILKE

THE TENTH ELEGY

O to be able, at the end of this grim realization,
to sing out rejoicing and praise to angels who'll take up my song.
O for not one of the clearly struck hammers of the heart
to ring false on a string that is slack or uncertain
or jangling. And that streaming tears may make my face
more dazzling: the mourning I've hidden, bloom.
O nights I have wronged, how beloved you'll be to me then.
Comfortless sisters, why didn't I accept you more
unquestioningly, bury my face more completely
in the hair you let down round your shoulders?
We, we squander our sorrows. We look
past them into the sadness of duration,
wondering if they'll end soon. But they're our
winter foliage, the dark evergreen of the psyche,
just one of the seasons of the hidden year – and not
only a season – a place, a fortress,
a couch, the ground, a residence.

Alas, the Sorrowtown streets are certainly strange
where, in a fake silence made from attempts to drown out,
knocked from the mould of emptiness the cast stands
boastful: hubbub gilded, a monument splitting.
How little trace he'd leave of his passage, some angel
that crushed underfoot their Market of Comfort
with the church at its edge, they bought ready made: it's spotless
and shut, disenchanted like a post-office on Sunday.
Outside though, the rims of the fair are rippling still.
Seesaws of freedom! Divers and jugglers of desire!
And the dolled-up figures on the Happiness shooting-stand:
when one of the more skilful hits, the pellet
rebounds from the mark, vanishing with
a tinny ring. He stumbles ahead, abandoning
acclaim for chance: for booths to entice every
curiosity are touting, drumming and blaring.

There's an even stranger spectacle, for grown-ups only:
the way money breeds, not just fun, but anatomical,
the sex life of money, complete with climax and foreplay –
it instructs and makes fertile . . .
But at the same time, out over there,
behind the last board, glued round with placards "Immortal",

where they vend a harsh beer that seems sweet if one can ever
be chewing fresh distractions to it . . . just
at the back of the plank, right behind it, it's *really* happening.
Children are playing, and lovers hold one another,
to one side, gravely, in the patchy grass,
and dogs mount and are mounted. The young fellow's
drawn on still further (perhaps he's in love with
a young Lament . . .) He follows her into the meadow.
She says "Far away. We live out there . . ."
                                        Where?
He goes after her, touched by her bearing,
her shoulders, her neck: she could be of noble stock.
But he turns away, leaves her then, looking back, nods . . .
What's the difference? She's only a Lament.

Only those who die young, in their first
birth into timeless indifference, unlearning of habits,
follow her lovingly. A girl
is waiting for them, befriends them, tenderly
shows them the things she has with her, pearls
of sorrow, the delicate veils of acceptance. She
goes with young men in silence.

But there, at their home in the valley,
One of the older Laments is ready to answer his questions:
"Once," she says, "we Laments were a great kindred.
"Our fathers mined there, among the great mountains.
"Now and again among humans you may find
"a smooth, polished fragment of sorrow ore,
"or drossy, petrified rage from an old volcano.
"They came from there. Once we were rich."

And gently she brings him through the far-stretching
landscapes of mourning, showing him the temple columns,
or the rubble of cities from which Emperor Laments
once ruled the country wisely;
showing him the high-branched weeping-trees
(known to the living only as delicate leafage);
showing him the creatures of sorrow, cropping the grass.
Often a bird is startled and, winging
flat past their raised faces, draws far away
the ideogram of his isolated cry.
At evening she takes him away to the graves
of the elders among the Lament-race, the sibyls and watchlords.
But as night falls, their steps grow more gentle,
and before long the moon rises,

ubiquitous, vigilant tombstone, akin to the lofty
Sphinx on the Nile, the
face on a speechless chamber.
And they stare at the crowned head
which, wordless, eternally lays
the face of men on the scales of the stars.

Dizzy from the recentness of death,
his look cannot grasp it. But their gaze
scares the owl out from the edge of the pschent
and, caressing the ripest-curve cheek
in a lengthy wingstroke, it softly
inscribes in his new dead hearing,
on two open pages,
the indescribable contour.

And above, the stars. New stars. Sufferingland
stars the Lament names slowly: "Here,
"look, the *Rider*, the *Rod*, the completer
"constellation they call *Wreathed Fruit*. Then,
"further away, toward the Pole: *Cradle*,
"*Way*, the *Burning Book*, *Doll*, *Window*
"But in the southern sky, pure as in the
"hollow of a holy hand, the clearly
"glittering *M* that stands for Mother."

But the dead man must go, and in silence the older
Lament leads him to the valley's cleft
where in the moonshine shimmers the spring
of joy. She speaks its name with reverence,
says "Among men
"it's a thundering stream."

They stand below the mountain ridge.
She embraces him. She is crying.

He takes his way alone up into the mountains
of original sorrow. Not once does a footstep resound
from his soundless fate.

But were the irrevocably dead to stir
us with an image, think, they would probably point
to the catkins pendulent on the leafless hazel,
or would think of rain as it damps
the dark realm of earth early on in the year.

And we, who think of happiness
rising, would have the emotion
that almost over-
whelms us when happiness
falls.

FROM THE CROATIAN OF NIKOLA ŠOP

PRAISE OF ROOSTERS

I: They appear . . .

I've lost all track
of time when in the distant
solitude the wharves begin to murmur
and, turning by chance towards the empty bed,
I think, with a smile:
sometimes it's really very hard
to go to bed alone, completely alone.

Silence.
All at once a lonely cry,
far off, wild and brimming freshness.
I can't tell who, or by whose house.
It shatters my thoughts, cracks the infinite
black slab of silence, as if a pearl-encrusted
chalice shattered. After it, as if
by previous arrangement, from innumerable
unseen places anchored on
the open sea of night, waiting for day,
strong, unanimous the answers chime
with dewy resonance, like pipes made from
young willow wands. They echo everywhere,
springing up closer and closer, one by one,
strange, lonely sounds. As they come nearer, there
are fewer of them, as if, frightened by
my study light, in silent water dews
were quenched.

Then just one more, unexpected, right beneath
my window. They cry full-throated, so that a
shiver runs right through me. Ringing, triumphant,
their voices leaving behind only a flicker
of hot steam, like an echo of the silence.

I know, I know. It's the cocks, one after the other,
I could tell by the one beneath my window.
Now's the time they call to each other
on their unending journey, call
so that they won't get lost, scorned
and forgotten guardians of the city's edge.

Robert Crawford

FROM THE GERMAN OF PAUL CELAN

1

FROST, EDEN

TintLaun:
a mune spreids amang rashes;
wi us, frostit tae daith
aa gits rid-het an sees.

It sees, wi a gliss
Fae yird-een.
Thi nicht, thi nicht, thi scharpit wattirs.
It sees, the E-wean.

It sees, it sees, we see,
Ah see ye, ye see me.
Frost'll be resureckit
afore thi fyne o this hour.

2

IN PRAG

Yon Hauf-daith,
bloatit wi oor sookit virr,
ligged roon us, ashvive –

an we
bevvied oan, twa sawl-crossit dirks,
tackit tae heivinstanes, leidbluid-bairns
in thi nichtcot

mair an mair
we goat intermelled, whit
drave us noo
nemless (wan o hoo mony
an thirty wiz ma vivual scaddaw
scrauchlin up naethin tae ye?)

203

broch
thi Haufyin erectit naewhaur,
yon Hradshin
Aureate fae thi smiddy o Naw,

bane-Yiddish,
dinged tae froe,
ran thru thi hourgless
doon whilk we swam, jist twa swevins, ringin
agin thi time, doon thi squers.

W. N. Herbert

SONNET

Thow, wha thru ma een thirls til thi hert
an twirls ma harns frae thir hanlawile dirr,
luke til th'agenbite o aa ma daeins
Amour stramashis wi merlineous ayns,

an gaes reivin roond wi sic a muckil virr
ut sparts ma sackliss spreits tae ivry airt,
till yae wae figour i thi toalbooth stauns
peeried o stevin but dowie o blairt:

this pith-proab Luve, that's dung me doon,
frae yir donsy een's sae eidently sped
ut's nithert me wi a fletch i thi flank;

uts straucht crunt's cut wi thi prime o puin,
girlean thi chitteran saul lyk a gled,
luke: thi deid hert crines i thi left-loof's hank.

AS IT MUST

O fae far-hie-an-atour gin yi waant
ut lyk thon, but ut's a blinnin haar
an thi scaldachans ur jist as tint that
hop frae brainch tae twig fur thi trace.

Life gaes oan as ut maun in perpetuity,
dithirs uts mony burns. An mithir's jist
pangan thi bairns wi breid, an stokan
thi bleeze anaa: thi darg scoors by, fu

or toom; thi arbitrary veesitur's
aff, snaa faas, mebbe ut brichtens up
or thon smirr that dwaums wintir durrs
tints, sogs yir shoon an frock, nicht faas.

Ut's no much, but therr's nae sign o mair:
thon path wisnae tae us, an frae anithir.

205

Glossary

This glossary makes no pretensions to be anything other than a help to reading Scots (including the Shetland Scots of W. J. Tait), for those who are not familiar with the language. Definitions have been kept to a bare minimum. Many difficulties arise from spelling which reflects pronunciation. It is worth remembering that there are often several alternative spellings for a given word (e.g. *toom, tuim, tume*). In many cases only the vowel is different from a related English word (e.g. *sair = sore; main = moan*), and often an English consonant is omitted (*loo = love; freen = friend*). In general, Scots gerund ends in -in, present participle in -an, and past participle in -it or -t. In some cases the Scots word is virtually identical to the French. For further information, consult the *Concise Scots Dictionary*, edited by Mairi Robinson (Aberdeen University Press, 1985).

aafie, awful
abeen, above
abeigh, aloof
abies, also
ablow, below
abuin, above
ae, one
aefald, aefellt, singleminded
aeth, oath
agait, on the road
agenbite, remorse
agley, awry
aiblins, perhaps
airt, point of the compass
aiss, ash
aizle, ember, glow
aiverin, eager
ajee, wide of the mark
allemand, orderly
alunt, alight
ane, one
anent, about
anerlie, only
arselins, backwards
ashet, dish
ashvive, alive as an ash
athil, noble
athin, within
athoot, without

athort, across
atour, about
aucht, due
auld-farrant, old-fashioned
ava, at all
awkwart, across
ayebydan, eternal
ayn(d), breath

bade, stayed
baess, cattle
baigit, begged
bairn(ie), child
bane-rife, full of bones
bap, bread roll
barm, ferment
bauchle, old shoe
bawbee, small coin
begoud, began
begrutten, tear-stained
behufis, behoves
beilin, suppurating
bekend, familiar
beld, bald
benmaist, innermost
bere, barley
besprent, scattered
bestial, cattle
bever, waver

bevvy, drink
bield, protect
bienly, comfortably
biggin, building
birl, whirl
birssy, bristling
bizz, bustle
blad, page, blast of wind
blaffert, squall
blairt, outburst
blane, blemish
blate, timid, dull
blawp, heave up water
blear, misty
blee, complexion
bleezed, drunk
blink, moment
blinlans, blindly
blinter, gleam
blye, happy
bogle, spirit
boke, vomit
bomulloch, (laugh) on the other side of one's face
bore, gap in clouds
borneheid, impetuous
boss, hollow
bot, without
bouk, body
boulie, bandy
brace, mantelpiece
brack, brine
braird, germinate
brash, beat
brayn-wud, stark-mad
braxy, salted sheep-meat
braw(lie), fine
bree, brew
breears, eyelashes
breel, move swiftly
breenge, rush
breve, book
brockie, badger
brod, board
brose, porridge
browden, think fondly
bruit, rumour

buik, bulk
buird, table
bumbazeit, dazzled
bumlick, stumbling block
buskit, adorned
buss, mass, clump
but baid, without hesitation
bygae, pass
bygaun, passing
bylins, by the way
byng, pyre
bystart, bastard

cackie, shit
cadie, cap
callan(t), young man
caller, fresh
camsteerie, perverse
canny, careful, pleasant
cantie, cheerful
cantrip, spell, magic
cassay-stane, cobble stone
cassent, faded
cauldruif, chill
cavaburd, blizzard
channer, grumble
chap, knock
chaumer, room
chief, intimate
chiel, lad, man
clachan, hamlet
clanjamfrie, company, rabble
clarsach, harp
cleckin, brood
cleg, horsefly
clek, language, talk
cleugh, chasm, valley
clint, cliff
cloor, blow
clout, cloth(e)
cluif, hoof
coft, bought
cog, pail
coof, fool
coopit, closed in
coorie, crouch
coorse, stormy

coost, cast
copt, overturned
corbie, crow
cot(ton), cottage
coup, capsize, quaff
couthy, pleasant, friendly
cowit, cropped
cra, crow
craapen, bent with age
crack, chat
craig, neck
craik, cry, croak
crang, body, esp. dead body
creeshie, greasy, oily
crine, cryne, shrivel, dry
crockle, cough
crouse, content
crowdie, soft cheese
crunt, blow
cuddy, horse
cuist, cast

daff, fool about
dale, part
daala-reek, mist
dander, wander
darg, work
da streen, yesterday
daud, blow
de, dee, die
dee, do
deave, deafen
deid, dead, death
deray, disturbance
derf, taciturn
dern, hide, hiding
dernlike, secret
deval(l), stop, rest, descend
ding, bang
dint, blow
dirdum, tumult
dirl, vibrate
dirr, daze, blur
disjaskit, disjointed
disparple, scatter
dock(en) (not a), not a bit
dock, arse

dodd, discomfit
doilsome, sorrowful
donner, daze
donsy, lovely
doo, pigeon, dove
dook, bathe
dool, dule, grief, pain
doon-moued, depressed
douce, sweet, respectable
doulie, sad
doup-scud, slap on the back-side
dour, hard, stern
dovers, dozes
dowd, faded, withered
dowf, dull, feeble
dowie, dismal, gloomy
downa, cannot
doazent, dozent, dazed
draigle, drag
drang, pull tight
dredgie, dirge
dree, drie, suffer
dreich, dreary
drizzen, moan
drouk, drench
drouth, dryness
drowie, indistinct
drucken, drunk
dub, pool
dubie, obscure
duds, clothes
dunner, bang, knock
dunt, thud, blow
durr, deaden
dwablie, feeble
dwaible, totter
dwalm, dwam(in), dwaum, swoon, dream
dwyne, wither

eem, float like a vapour
eer, reddish stain
eident, busy, keen
eisenin, lustful
eld, old age
ent, pay attention to
erd-din, earthquake

ere, early
ettle, to aim, purpose, guess

faa, who
fae, from
fael, sod of turf
fan, when
fain, loving
fairheid, beauty
fairin, deserts
fank, pen, enclosure
fankle, ensnare
farden, farthing
far-hie-an-atour, far off
fash, to trouble
fashious, caresome
faur, where
fecht, fight
feddit, faded
fell, strong(ly), loud(ly)
felloun, cruel
ferlie, *ferly*, portent, wonder
fey, crazy, fated
fient a, never a
fiere, comrade, brother
firk, jerk out
fisk, fart
firtae, in order to
fit, what
flaughter, flame
fleer, *flare*, mock
fleg, *fley*, frighten
fletch, arrow
flichter, flutter
flim, mist
flownrie, fragile
flype, flay, tear, turn inside out
foost, rot
forbye, near, beside
fordel, advance
forduin, exhausted
forenen(s)t, in front of
forestem, prow
forfairn, tired out
forfaut, sin
forfoch(t)en, exhausted
forhon, forgive

forvagt, wandered
forwandert, weary
fou, full, drunk
fouth, abundance
fouthless, barren
fracaw, squabble
fraim, stranger
fraucht, load
frazit, dismayed
freit, omen
fremmit, *fremt*, estranged, strange
frichtifie, frighten
froe, semen
fuddrie-leam, flash of lightning
fullyeries, foliage
furthshaw, show
furth-sprent (streckit), widespread
fute hait, straightway
fyke, fusser
fyle, to dirty
fyne, end

gaff, guffaw
gairit, patched
gait, *gate*, way, road
glalshoch, titbits
gang, go
gangrel, vagabond, outcast
gar, to cause, make
gash, pale
geal, freeze
geck, look
genetrice, female parent
gerss, grass
gesserant, brilliant
gey, very
gif, *geiff*, if, though
gimmer, young ewe
girl, scare
girn, complain
glaikit, dazed, stupid
glammer, conjure
glansin, brightening
glaum, rave
glaur, mud
gled, hawk
gleg, quick

gleid, spark, flame
glent, glance
gliff, glimpse
glink, glint
glisk, gliss, glimpse
glyte, cockeyed
golloch-skartit, insect-scratched
gousterous, boisterous
gove, stair
gowk, fool, cuckoo
gowl, cleft, gully
gowl, to howl
gowp, swallow, gape
graen, groan
graith, apparatus, prepare
graim, grame, grief, grieve
greikin, dawn
greit, greet, grett, weep, tears
grieshoch, glowing embers, flame-
    less fire
grue, shudder
grugous, ugly
grumph(ie), pig
gruntle, muzzle
grup, catch
guerdon, recompense
guff, smell
guffie, stupid
gurl, gurgle
gusty, tasty
gyte, mad

haar, mist
haase, throat
haffits, hair
hailie, holy
haill, whole
hailyer, hawlers
hain, keep, preserve
hairst, harvest
hait, atom, particle
hale hypothec, everything
handsel, gift
hangie, not too well
hank, side-chest
hanlawhile, momentary
hantle, quantity

hap, chance, cover
hap, hap-lace, knitted shawl
hapshackellit, hobbled
harl, pull
harberie, herbrie, harbour
harn, brain
haroosh, tumult
haud his wisht, be silent
hauflin, youth
haun, hand
haus, neck
hazel-raw, lichen
hechyuch, hawking
heeze, hoist up
heich, high
hertscaud, heartbreak
heuch, steep
hidlins, hidden
hinnie, term of endearment
hirple, limp
hirsel, flock
hoch, thigh
hod, hide
hotter, bubbling, seething
houff, howff, shelter, tavern
houlat, owl
howdlins, secretly
howe, plain river valley
howk, dig, hollow
huggert, serrated
hunkers (on his), squatting
hurdies, haunches
hure, whore
hyne, far

ilk(a), each, every
ill-deedie, mischievous
ill-yaise(d), ill-use(d)
in-ben, within
inch, island
intermell, mingle

jalouse, suspect, guess
jimp, close, graceful
jink, dodge
jouk, trick
jow, ring, shake

210

kebbuck, cheese
keek, peep
keelie, rough, a street-arab
keethanlie, apparently
kendlit, conceived
kennle, kindle
kenspeckle, distinctive, recognisable
kent, staff
kinrick, kingdom
kist, chest, coffin
kittle, tickle
knap, knee
knock, clock
knowe, hill
knurly, knotted
kythe, appear
kything, vision, manifestation

laich, laigh, low, modest
lair, grave
laith, loath
laivrick, lark
lane, alone
lap, leapt
lappit, flap
lauch, laugh
laun, land
lave, rest, remainder
lawlie, humble
lea, leave
leal, loyal
leam, shine
lee, lie
lee-lang, life-long, all day through
leet, list
left-loof, left hand
leid, language, song
levin-fire (flaucht), lightning
lief, willing
liefu-lane (its), all alone
lift, sky
ligg, lie
limmer, rogue, prostitute
lippen, trust
lipper, leper
lire, surface

lither, sluggish
lodden, load
loo, love
loof, hand
loon, loun, fellow, rogue, youth
lowch, slouch
lowe, flame
lown, quiet
lowp, loup, leap
lowse, release
lucken, gripped
lug, ear
luift, sky
lunt, burn
lunye, loin
lusum, lovesome
luttard, bent
lyart, grey-haired
lykewauk-kimmer, deathbed comforter
lyood, sound

maist, almost
maen, moan
maik, mate
makar, poet
mallie, fulmar
man, maun, must
mapamound, world
mauchtless, limp, helpless
maw, seagull
mawk, maggot
meeth, mark
mell, mingle
mense, sense
merchless, infinite
merlineous, hawklike
merrit, married
messan tyke, cur
mind, mine, remember
minnie, mother
mirk, dark
mirligae, spindle
mochiness, dampness
moedoo, meadow
mool, earth, grave
moose-eab, cobweb

211

mou, mouth
mowdie, mole
my lane, alone

nain, own
nate, purpose
nearhaun, close by
neb, nose, face
ned, horse
neddar, adder
neeb, nod
neive, hand
nesh, delicate
neuk, corner
nicher, whinny
nickit, stolen
nither, pinch, freeze
noen, hum
norlan, north(ern)
nowt, ox

onding, downpour
onfall, attach, disease
ongaun, rowdy behaviour
on flocht, in terror
ontil, to
onwittand, not knowing
onwrokyn, unavenged
onwyte, await
onygate, anywhere
oorie, dismal
ootlin, alien
or, before
or than, or else
outbock, let loose
outbullyrand, gushing out
owregang, cross
owreharle, pull over

Pace, Easter
paiks, deserts
pang, stuff
park, field
parpane, parapet
parritch-spirtle, porridge stirrer
pawmie, strike on the palm
pech, sigh, breathe hard

peelie-wallie, pale
peerie, little, to reduce; humming-top
perjink, exact
pine, pain
pith-proab, piercing
plainstane, flagstone
pleep, call (of a bird)
pleiter, paddle
pliskie, escapade
ploy, joke, undertaking
plunk, to desert
poke, bag
poulet-ree, henrun
poulp, octopus
powe, head
pree, *prieve*, taste
preen, pin
press, cupboard
puckle, a little

queyne, girl
quhidder, tremble
quhile, while
quhou, how
quidna, could not

radgie, mad
raff and ree, easily and freely
ramfeezle, confused
ramp(ish), wild
ramskeerie, restless, irresponsible
ramstam, headlong
raucle, rough
rave, tore, cut
rax, reach, stretch
redd, clear
ree, tipsy
reekie, smoky
reeshle, splash
reive, rob
rerd, shouting
ressave, receive
reuch(lik), rough
rift, belch
riggin, roof
rin like stour, run very fast

212

rive, split
rodden, rowan(berry)
roesse, praise
rooky, misty
rouch-rider, rough-rider
rouchlin, rough
roun, talk quietly
row, wrap
routh, rowth, plenty, rich
rug, tug, pull
runkle, creese, wrinkle
runt, trunk, stump
ruth, pity
rypit, bereft

sackless, saikless, feeble, innocent
sain, bless
sair, sorely
sair, to serve
sair-saucht, desired
sangschaw, concert
sark, shirt, shift
sauch, willow; sigh
savendie, intelligence
savendle, stable
saw, sow
sca'd, scabby
scaddaw, shadow
scaldachan, fledgling
scantlin, little
scart, scratch
scathe, damage, hurt
scaur, rock
scherpit, sharpened
schire, bright
s(c)hauchle, shuffle
scho, she
sclater, wood-louse
sclent, sklent, glance sideways
sclim, climb
scoor, hurry
scoutherie, rainy
scoyan, twisting
scraith, scream
scrieve, scryve, screive, write
scrim, coarse linen
scruntie, stunted

scunner, disgust
sculdudry, fornication
scurl, sore
seamaw, seagull
seelfu, serene
seich, sigh
sey(e), try
seyll, contentment
shanker, tumour
shelpit, thin
sheylit, distraught
shiv, knife
sho(o)g, swing, shake
showd, swing
sibbit, closely related
sic(can), such
siccar, sure(ly)
sicwyse, in such a way
skail, scatter, strong wind
skair, share, reef
skaith, harm, wound
skald, bard
skeery, irresponsible
skellum, rascal
skelloch, scream
skelp, strike, rattle
skiftin, shower
skinkle, glitter
skire, skyre, bright
skirl, cry, wind
skite, slide, throw
skouk, skulk
skraugh, shrieked
skreak-o-dawin, break of day
skruckenil, shrunken
slee, slyly
slidder, slippery
slock, extinguish
sloom, slip
smeddum, spirit
smert, pain
smirr, thin rain
smittle, infections
smorit, smothered
smoor, smore, gradually die, extinguish
smutler, nibbler

snaw-wreithe, snowdrift
sneeshin, snuff
snek, snatch
snell, bitter
sog, soak
soom, soum, swim
souch, sigh
soukit, sucked
spae, spell, prophecy
spaeman, prophet
spale, splinter
spart, scatter
speir, ask
speug, sparrow
sprachle, sprawl
sprent, sprinkle
stank, pond
stark, strong
start, disturb
straun, strand
steeny, stony
steer, stirring
steek, steik, shut
steekit, closed
stekit, pierced
stell, fix
stent, to stop, allotted task
stevin, voice
stieve, hard
stishie, commotion
stoggit, pitted
stoor (rin like), run very fast
stot, bounce
stoond, stound, throb, pang
stour, battle
stramash, uproar
stravaig, wander
stret, tight
strone, piss
suckle, sickle
sumph, fool
swack, supple
swa(i)ver, totter
swaw, wave
swee, swing
sweel, wash
sweer/sweir(t), reluctant, tired

swelly, swallow
swickerie, fraud
swither, hesitate
sych, sigh
synd(e), wash
syne, then, since
syver, ditch

tack, tie
taigle, (en)tangle
tash, stain
teem, pour, empty
teen, anger, grief
tent, care
thak, thatch
thir, this, these
thirl, pierce, hold in bondage
thocht, as though
thole, suffer
thon, that
thonder, yonder
thowless, listless
thrang, busy
thriep, argue
thwankan, mingling in thick and
    gloomy procession (used of
    clouds)
til, to
timmer, beat, thrash
timmit, drained
tine, tyne, lose
tink, fellow
tirrick, tern
toalbooth, jail
toom, empty
toonmals, in-fields
toorie, a knob for a cap
tourbillioun, whirlwind
towmond, twelve-month
traik, weary, to roam
tramort, corpse
trauchle, to labour
trauchlet, exhausted
trig, neat
trock, business
trummle, tremble
tuim, empty

tuim-neived, empty handed
turngree, staircase
turs, carry away
twa-faald, bent double
tyauve, strive

ugsome, repulsive
unkent, unknown
unsiccar, unsteady
upskail, rise up
ure, haze, suffocating heat

vaig, wander
vaudy, proud
vennel, alley
virr, energy
vivual, living
vyre, outstanding person

wabbit-out, exhausted
wae, wretched
waement, lament
waik, care
wairsh, bitter
wame, belly
wanrestit, restless
wardis, rooms
warstle, wrestle
watter-crow, water-blackbird
waumle, turn over
waur, worse
wean, baby
weazand, wizened

wede awa, faded away
ween, wind
weird, fate
wersh, bitter
weym, belly
whaup, curlew
wheesht, be quiet
wheen, few
whiles, at times
whilk, which
whitrick, weasel
wick, bay
win, come, reach
winnock, window
wir, our
wis, desire
wod, wood, mad
won, win
wrokin, revenged
wuddreme, confusion
wynd, lane
wyte, blame, fault

yaff, contemptible person
yare, yearning
yeld, barren
yett, gate
yin, one
yird(ly), earth(ly)
yerdin, yirdin, burial
yock, shut
yowdendrift, snowdrift
yowe, eye
yowther, smoke

INDEX OF TRANSLATORS

216

INDEX OF POETS TRANSLATED
(With first lines/titles of originals)